p. 164 Blend

ISBN Number 0-913916-10-2
Library of Congress catalog number 74-18906

Printed in Nashville, Tennessee
United States of America

Pumpkins,
Pinwheels,
and
Peppermint
Packages

Learning
Centers
and
Activities
to make
every day
a
special day.

From:
Imogene Forte
Mary Ann Pangle
Robbie Tupa

DEDICATION AND ACKNOWLEDGMENTS

This book is dedicated to teachers who believe that from the first hello in September to the last goodbye in June, every school day can be a special day,

...and to all the other adults who direct children's learning and believe that learning can continue to be creatively challenging and exciting.

To Patty Pangle, who gave up her precious summer vacation for completion of this project, we extend our sincere thanks. Her unique artistic flair, and fanciful interpretation of the authors' ideas and purposes, is creatively reflected in the double-page illustrations for the thirty-eight learning centers and the book's title page.

Special acknowledgment is gratefully accorded to Mrs. Bobbie Grubb, typist, critic and friend, whose contribution to this effort has been boundless.

Other Kids' Stuff books:

Center Stuff for Nooks, Crannies and Corners
Complete Learning Centers for the Elementary Classroom
  Imogene Forte, Mary Ann Pangle and Robbie Tupa

Cornering Creative Writing
Learning Centers, Games, Activities and Ideas for
the Elementary Classroom
  Imogene Forte, Mary Ann Pangle and Robbie Tupa

Creative Math Experiences for the Young Child
  Imogene Forte and Joy MacKenzie

Creative Science Experiences for the Young Child
  Imogene Forte and Joy MacKenzie

Kids' Stuff, Kindergarten and Nursery School
  Mary Jo Collier, Imogene Forte and Joy MacKenzie

Kids' Stuff, L. P. Activity Record with Guide for
Teachers and Parents

Kids' Stuff, Math
Activities, Games and Ideas for the Elementary Classroom
  Marjorie Frank

Kids' Stuff, Reading and Language Experiences
Intermediate – Jr. High
  Imogene Forte, Marjorie Frank and Joy MacKenzie

Kids' Stuff, Reading and Spelling, Primary Level
  Mary Jo Collier, Imogene Forte and Joy MacKenzie

Nooks, Crannies and Corners
Learning Centers for Creative Classrooms
  Imogene Forte and Joy MacKenzie

Published by – Incentive Publications
Box 12522
Nashville, Tennessee 37212

PREFACE

The 38 learning centers and more than 350 activities in <u>Pumpkins, Pinwheels and Peppermint Packages</u> have been compiled to help boys and girls understand and appreciate American holidays and customs and make learning fun.

Each learning center is completely illustrated and contains:

(1) Activities in the following academic areas...
    Communications (Language Arts)
    Creative Arts (Art and Music)
    Environmental Studies (Social Studies and Science)
    Quantitative Experience (Math)
(2) A puzzle or game
(3) A smorgasboard of "just for fun" ideas

The centers have been kept as flexible and open-ended as possible. They have been planned to be effectively implemented in both in and out of school programs. Many of the activities will lend themselves to use in church schools, day care centers, camps, scouting, and a variety of other settings.

Probably no two groups will use any model center in this book in exactly the same way. In rare instances the entire center plan may be adaptable to a given situation. Many times, however, it may be desirable to use only a part or parts of a given center. Sometimes selected activities may be combined with basal or other text related materials; teachers will often find them to be companionable and supportive to directed teaching sessions. At other times they may be used by individual students on a contract or free choice basis. Even individual activities within the centers have been structured to "stand alone" to give teachers the widest possible range of choices in selection and presentation. Hopefully, their actual implementation will be as creative and as spontaneous as each teacher's imagination and adaptation.

The listing of books for students (Appendix, Part 2) includes resource books for the centers as well as books for enrichment and recreational reading. They are listed in the order of the centers' appearance in the book, and have been carefully selected to make the activities instructionally exciting.

We hope that you will mix and match, take from and add to, and adjust the activities to meet your unique needs, and that Pumpkins, Pinwheels and Peppermint Packages will indeed help to make every day a special day for you and yours.

Imogene Forte
Mary Ann Pangle
Robbie Tupa

Nashville, Tennessee
September, 1974

TABLE OF CONTENTS

PREFACE 5

LEARNING CENTERS

SEPTEMBER
   First Day of School — Grand Opening................. 16
      Crazy Classrooms (Imaginary story writing)
      Portrait Pals (Drawing portraits)
      Pick and Choose (Democratic planning)
      Meter Maids (Meters and centimeters)
      Friendship (Making friends game)
      Just for Fun

   First Day of Autumn — Actually Autumn................ 22
      Leaf Limericks (Writing limericks)
      Indian Summer (Illustrating Indian Summer)
      Color Changes (Experimenting with color)
      Leaf Detectives (Identifying leaves)
      Leaf Lovers (Leaf matching game)
      Just for Fun

   American Indian Day — Pow-wow...................... 28
      Smoke Signals (Sending messages)
      Chant Choice (Interpretative listening)
      Diary Diorama (Comparing life styles)
      Wigwam Worries (Problem solving)
      Bear Hunt (Game)
      Just for Fun

OCTOBER
   Columbus Day — Ship Ashore...................... 34
      Action Reporters (Creative writing)
      Sailors' Delight (Cardboard ship construction)
      Exploring the Unknown (Writing research reports)
      Map Makers (Making relief maps)
      Stay on Course (Phrase game)
      Just for Fun

Halloween – Halloween Heyday...................... 40
    Trick or Treat (Pantomiming)
    Bag It (Costume design)
    Pumpkin Parade (Plant growth)
    Scary Scene (Geometry)
    Ghost Getaway (Maze)
    Just for Fun

        Haunted House......................... 46
    Boo! Guess Who! (Writing riddles)
    Dreadful Dioramas (Making dioramas and writing
                open-ended stories)
    Silly Senses (Using the five senses)
    Enter and Escape (Problem solving)
    Witches' Hideout (Halloween game)
    Break the Spell (Crossword puzzle)
    Just for Fun

Fire Prevention Week – Sound the Alarm............. 50
    Hot Line (Writing a class newspaper)
    Bucket Brigade (Interpreting research findings)
    What's It All About? (Exploring community
                resources)
    Fire Hazards (Sketching home fire hazards)
    Screeching Sirens (Question and answer game)
    Just for Fun

NOVEMBER
Election Day – The Race Is On...................... 56
    Vote Getters (Writing jingles)
    Chore-a-thon (Staging a telethon)
    Campaign Gimmicks (Making campaign hats and
                buttons)
    Platform Writers (Developing a campaign
                platform)
    Hit the Trail (Mapping a campaign route)
    Puzzle Power (Crossword puzzle)
    Just for Fun

National Book Week – In A Bind...................... 62
    Play Day (Play productions)
    Jazz It Up (Book illustrations)
    TIM–B–r–r–r (Paper making process)
    Dewey Dares (Dewey Decimal game)
    All Parts Accounted For! (Crossword puzzle)
    Just for Fun

Thanksgiving – Turkey Tales...................... 68
    Yum Yum (Making a recipe book)
    The Big Show (Writing and presenting a puppet
                show)
    Big Builders (Constructing a village)
    Beginner Barters (Practicing bartering)
    Turkey Chase (Sentence game)
    Just for Fun

DECEMBER
    First Day of Winter – Deep Freeze.................. 74
    Snowflake Structure (Using descriptive words)
    Snowflake Swirl (Soap flake painting)
    Wintry Wonderland (Observing family activities)
    Cold Wave (Weather forecasting)
    Whiz Through Winter (Word puzzle)
    Just for Fun

Hanukkah – Dizzy Dreidel......................... 80
    Pic A Word (Creative story writing)
    Print Out (Potato printing)
    Candle Glow (Developing questions)
    Dreidel Spinners (Drawing circles)
    Gift Game (Spelling game)
    Just for Fun

Christmas – Santa's Spree......................... 86
    Santa's Shopping List (Writing sentences)
    Santa's Style Show (Designing clothes)
    Customs Kaleidoscope (Christmas customs)
    Tasty Trimmings (Planning and budgeting a
                Christmas dinner)
    Rudolph's Route (Maze)
    Just for Fun

Jingle Jangle.......................... 92
    Candy Canes (Writing phrases)
    Toyland Tizzy (Creating Santa's toys)
    Tempting Trees (Making bird feeders)
    Stocking Stuffers (Using money)
    Tree Trimming (Tree decorating game)
    Just for Fun

JANUARY
    New Year's Day - Midnight Madness................. 98
        Resolution Riters (Writing resolutions)
        Masquerade Ball (Mask construction)
        Notable New Years (Writing reports)
        New Year's Bowl (Developing multiplication and
                division skills)
        Ring In The New Year (Spelling game)
        Just for Fun

    Pun Week - Fun Puns............................. 104
        Pun-ished Players (Writing creative puns)
        Name Game (Illustrating puns)
        Phonic Phumbles (Deciphering puns)
        What's the Angle (Using mathematical terms)
        Fun Finders (Pun game)
        Just for Fun

    Birthdays - Cake Bake............................. 110
        Birthday Balloons (Creative writing)
        Just For You (Making birthday cards)
        Signs of the Time (Zodiac and horoscope signs)
        Party Time (Making a cake)
        Blow Out the Candles (Noun, verb and adjective
                game)
        Just for Fun

FEBRUARY
    Groundhog Day - Peek-A-Boo...................... 116
        Groundhog Gossip (Making creative story
                booklets)
        Shadow Show (Shadow play)
        Which Way? (Map reading)
        Cloudy or Clear (Weather)
        Underground Playground (Maze)
        Just for Fun

Abraham Lincoln's Birthday — Lincoln Lore........... 122
    Dear Abe (Letter writing)
    Peep Show (Cardboard carpentry)
    Wide World of Lincoln (Developing mental imagery)
    Math Whizzer (Problem construction)
    Match the Logs (Question and answer game)
    Just for Fun

Valentine's Day — Hearty Party..................... 128
    Poetry Pals (Writing poetry)
    Valentine Visions (Making collages)
    Hanging Hearts (Expressing emotions)
    Sweet Treats (Using a balance scale)
    Secret Senders (Missing letters game)
    King of Hearts (Game)
    Just for Fun

George Washington's Birthday — Washington Write-ups... 136
    Washington's Secret (Word meaning)
    Shape and Shade (Costuming)
    Worries and Wonders (Making inferences)
    Decoders Delight (Number coding)
    Mount Vernon Mystery (Crossword puzzle)
    Just for Fun

Dental Health Week — The Brush Off.................. 142
    Dental Describers (Using nouns and adjectives)
    The Big Bag (Paper bag puppetry)
    The Answer, Please (Using resource books)
    Fun Flossers (Graphing)
    Tooth Teasers (Crossword Puzzle)
    Just for Fun

Black History Week — Parade of Heroes............... 148
    Guessing the Guise (Writing and presenting reports)
    Musical Moods (Listening to music and writing
                        paragraphs)
    Tribal Tribute (Writing stories, plays or poems)
    Super Stars (Computing sport averages)
    Pyramid of Heroes (Pyramid puzzle)
    Just for Fun

MARCH

    Saint Patrick's Day — Leaping Leprechaun 154
        Kiss and Tell (Creative writing)
        Hide and Seek (Leprechaun murals)
        Emerald Isle (Imaginary travels)
        Greenery Graph (Bar graphing)
        Pot of Gold (Spelling game)
        Just for Fun

    First Day of Spring — Spring Whing Ding.............. 160
        Spring Sequence (Sequencing)
        Spring Signs (Making Mobiles)
        Spinning Seasons (The earth's revolution)
        Spring Spenders (Using money)
        Spring Blends (Phonics game)
        Just for Fun

    National Wildlife Week — Animal Critters............. 166
        Simile Sound Off (Writing similes)
        Animal Menageria (Drawing animals)
        Animal Exit (Studying extinct animals)
        Trips 'n Travels (Graphing bird migration)
        Sanctuary Safety (Animal identification game)
        Just for Fun

APRIL

    April Fool's Day — Foolish Fun...................... 172
        April Auction (Spelling)
        Fool Follies (Writing and producing plays)
        Timely Jokes (Using time lines)
        Fantastic Foolers (Using consumer marketing skills)
        Jokeville (Sentence game)
        Just for Fun

    Earth Week — Earth Rebirth.......................... 178
        Information Station (Letter writing)
        Rocks Renewed (Painting rocks)
        City Solutions (Drawing and studying a pollution
                    mural)
        Recycled Recipes (Illustrating recycling process)
        Pollution Pests (Pollution problem game)
        Just for Fun

Easter – Bunny Bonanza........................... 184
    Sunny Side Up (Creative writing)
    Scrambled Eggs (Making eggshell mosaics)
    Easter Parade (Studying Easter customs)
    Egg Estimaters (Estimating)
    Treasure Hunt (Treasure hunt game)
    Just for Fun

Arbor Day – Treasure Trees........................ 190
    Tree Talk (Writing dialogue)
    Shapely Silhouettes (Tree identification)
    Dig It (Planting a tree)
    Ring Count (Computing a tree's age)
    Plot the Spot (Matching game)
    Just for Fun

MAY
May Day – Flower Shower........................... 196
    Rhyme Review (Developing mental imagery)
    May Mystery (Paper construction)
    Flower Fair (Flower identification)
    May Day Madness (Charting time)
    May Mix–up (Word scramble game)
    Just for Fun

Mother's Day – Marvelous Moms.................... 202
    Miles of Smiles (Creative writing)
    A Day with Mother (Corsage making)
    Busy Moms (Mural production and pantomiming)
    Timetable Tally (Developing time schedules)
    Smiles and Flowers (Directions game)
    Just for Fun

Pickle Week – Pickle Puss.......................... 208
    Pickles on Parade (Writing advertisements)
    Pickle Production (Making a model pickle factory)
    Pickle Pickers (Investigating occupations)
    Nickel for A Pickle (Computing prices and weights)
    Pickle Patch (Game)
    Just for Fun

Last Day of School – Close Out...................... 214
    Our Gang (Compiling a class yearbook)
    Bird's Eye View (Making dioramas)
    Highlights (Creating a television program)
    Fun and Facts (Reviewing mathematical concepts)
    Guess Who (Clue game)
    Just for Fun

SUMMER FUN
Flag Day – Stars and Stripes........................ 220
    Talking Flags (Creating alphabet flags)
    Flag Designers (Designing a class flag)
    Flag Wavers (Displaying a flag)
    Flag Factories (Using numerical computation skills)
    Pennant Play (International numeral pennant game)
    Just for Fun

Father's Day – Pops are Tops........................ 226
    Dad Diorama (Making dioramas)
    Fathers Unlimited (Drawing portraits)
    Job Market (Career description)
    Vital Statistics (Averaging)
    Job Market (Crossword puzzle)
    Just for Fun

First Day of Summer – The Heat's On................. 232
    Travel Bureau (Writing travel reports)
    Big Dip (Creating underwater scenes)
    Nation Location (Investigating climatic conditions)
    Heat Wave (Using common measurements)
    Vacation Travels (Map game)
    Just for Fun

Fourth of July – The Big Bang....................... 238
    Patriotic Poets (Writing poetry)
    Fancy Fireworks (Creating make-believe fireworks)
    Real Researchers (Making oral reports)
    Pack Your Basket (Using money)
    Passing Parade (Parade game)
    Just for Fun

A VERY PRACTICAL APPENDIX

1. WREATH OF ACHIEVEMENT...................... 245

2. BULLETIN BOARDS
   September Scene........................... 247
   October Fright............................ 248
   Remember November......................... 249
   December Delights.........................250
   January Joy Ride.......................... 251
   February Favorites........................ 252
   March is Breezin' in...................... 253
   April All Around Us.......................254
   Magical May............................... 255
   Summer Sun Fun............................ 256

3. ANSWERS FOR PUZZLES AND QUIZZES.......... 257

4. BOOKS FOR STUDENTS........................ 263

5. SELECTED TEACHER REFERENCES.............. 281

Portrait Pals
draw a fellow classmate
crazy classroom
write a story
School
Invent a subject
create a holiday
visit the future
art
My new subject is . . .

1st
of
chool

Pick
and
Choose

Vote

vote for favorite

your subject

Meter
Ed Maids
Ann Tom Phil
Steve
Sue

measure your
height in
meters

I vote for
math

The first day of school is often
times eagerly anticipated on one hand,
and dreaded on the other,
by both students and teachers.
This of all days should be a happy one, full of
satistying experiences.

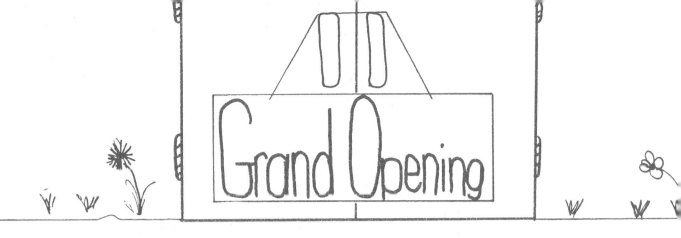

CENTER PURPOSES:

> After completing this center, the
> student should develop motivation
> and enthusiasm for the first day
> of school through learning experiences
> in comparative measurement,
> democratic planning, creative
> writing, and art.

CENTER ACTIVITIES:

Communications

"Crazy Classrooms"

Instruct the students to use one of the following ideas to create
an imaginary story to be read aloud at story-sharing time:

Invent a new school subject.

Be teacher for a day.

Create a new school holiday.

The class votes for the teacher to purchase a homework
machine.

A visit to a school of the future.

Creative Arts

"Portrait Pals"

Utilize student-produced portraits to encourage verbal
interaction and to help individuals within the group to become
better acquainted. Provide art supplies to enable the students
to draw portraits of new classmates they would like to know
better. Each student can be identified then through a guessing
game centering on a study of the portraits.

Environmental Studies

"Pick and Choose"

To encourage participation in the development of a democratic classroom environment, prepare a ballot for each student. List the school subjects, daily schedule, and classroom jobs. Ask the students to check their favorite subject, reorganize the daily schedule, and vote for one job they would like.

After the ballots have been marked and placed in the ballot box, a committee may tally the votes and report the election results to the class.

The follow-up discussion should provide a lively setting for clarification and extension of concepts related to the democratic election system.

Quantitative Experience

"Meter Maids"

Place meter and yardsticks in the center. On a chart print instructions for students to use as they measure each other and compare their height in meters and centimeters and in feet and inches. Provide graph paper for the students to use to record the results.

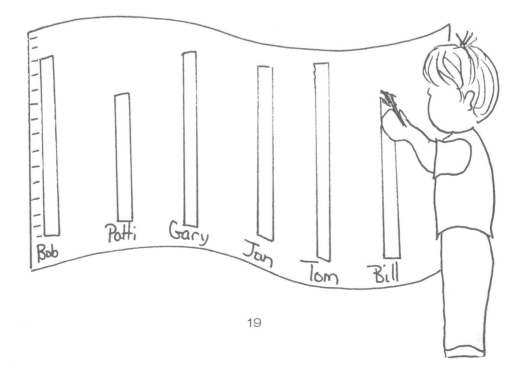

"Friendship"

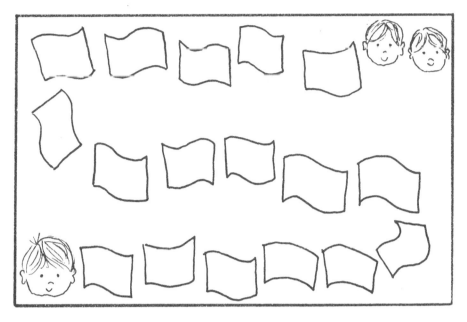

Preparation Directions:

1. Enlarge the game board on tagboard.
2. Using strips of tagboard, write the following phrases:

> My favorite pet is _____ . Move one space.
> I like to eat _____ . Move two spaces.
> There are _____ people in my family. Take another turn.
> I am _____ years old. Lose one turn.
> I have attended this school _____ years. Move one space.
> My favorite school subject is _____ . Take another turn.
> I like to play _____ . Move two spaces.
> One of my hobbies is _____ . Move one space.
> The television program I like best is _____ . Lose one turn.
> School is fun because _____ . Move three spaces.

3. Provide two markers.

Player Directions:

1. Each player selects a marker and places it on the game board.
2. The cards are shuffled and placed face down. Taking turns, players draw a card, answer the question, and move the number of spaces indicated.
3. The first player to reach the two friends wins the game.

JUST FOR FUN

Ask the students to use pictures cut from magazines to make a classroom collage depicting their summer activities. A discussion of the similarities and differences of the summer activities will help members of the group become better acquainted. (The sensitive teacher will want to lead this discussion to help boys and girls who spent the summer in their own backyards feel that their summer experiences were as exciting and merit sharing just as much as those of their widely traveled classmates.)

Provide art supplies for each student to make their own name tag. Shuffle all the name tags and pin one name tag on each student's back. Each student must then find the classmate that matches the name on his back, through clues given him by his classmates.

Write a letter to your new students welcoming them to their brand new classroom.

Divide the class into small groups and give each student a wooden ice cream spoon to be used as a puppet. Provide art supplies for faces to be drawn on the spoon and for hair and clothing to be added. Ask the students to use the puppets to tell about themselves.

The students might enjoy playing a recall game. After forming a circle, one student is chosen to be the "pointer" and stands in the center. He then points to another player and before the count of ten the chosen player must identify the name of the "pointer". If he guesses correctly, he exchanges places with the "pointer".

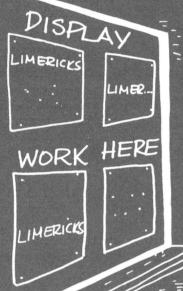

COLOR WHEEL
MOUNT LEAVES ON TREE AND CLASSIFY THEM . . .
MAPLE
BOOKS

CENTER PURPOSES:

> After completing this center, the student should develop appreciation and understanding of autumn through learning experiences in creating limericks, experimenting with color, identifying geometric shapes, and art.

CENTER ACTIVITIES:

Communications

"Leaf Limericks"

A limerick is a nonsense poem of five lines with a particular kind of rhythm or meter. For student motivation, read some limericks and provide group direction for composing limericks to be written on the chalk board. Instruct the students to write a limerick about a leaf. Then provide additional time for writing limericks about autumn. Supply art materials to be used to illustrate the limericks before displaying them on an attractively prepared bulletin board.

Creative Arts

"Indian Summer"

Indian Summer comes in late October or early November, and it is a period when fair weather and warm days can be expected. There are many stories concerning the origin of Indian Summer. We do know that the American Indians looked forward to and enjoyed Indian Summer. Provide resource books and lead a group discussion to enable the students to gain understanding of the Indian Summer season.

Divide a roll of white shelf paper into sections and place the paper and crayons in a quiet corner of the room. Instruct the students to illustrate one of the following ideas:

How the Indians celebrated Indian Summer

What causes Indian Summer

One idea of the origin of Indian Summer

Indian Summer activities of today

Share the pictures by using an opaque projector to project the pictures on a screen or on the wall.

Environmental Studies

"Color Changes"

Provide resource books to enable the students to understand why leaves turn different colors in autumn. Instruct the students to write a short report explaining this chemical process. As a follow-up activity, prepare a table with water colors and paper for color experiments.

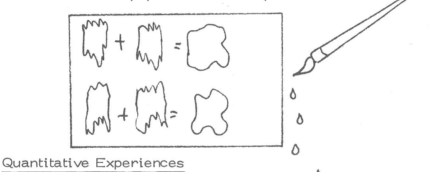

Quantitative Experiences

"Leaf Detectives"

Take the class on a field trip to collect beautiful autumn leaves. Assist the students in mounting and identifying the leaves. Instruct the students to find geometric shapes in each leaf and label the mounted leaves accordingly.

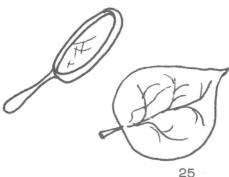

25

"Leaf Lovers"

Preparation Directions:

1. Using forty index cards, draw pictures of twenty different leaves (drawing the same picture on two cards). Print the name of the leaf on each card.

2. On six cards draw a picture of a tree.

3. Two players may play this game.

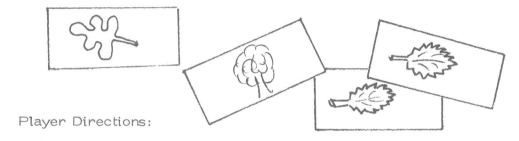

Player Directions:

1. Shuffle the cards and deal all the cards.

2. The players are not to look at their cards. The first player lays a card down; then the second player lays a card down. If the second player's card matches the first player's card, he takes all the cards that have been played. If the card does not match, the players continue to lay cards down until a match has been made.

3. When a card with a tree is played, it is considered a lucky card and can be played for any card.

4. The game is continued until one player runs out of cards.

5. The person with the most cards wins the game.

JUST FOR FUN

The following topics might serve as ideas for creative stories:

The leaf who was afraid of falling off the tree

How the leaves felt as boys and girls stepped on them

The life cycle of a leaf

What happened the night Jack Frost painted the leaves

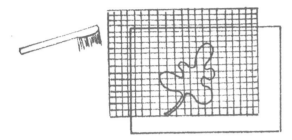

Provide a small square of screen wire, tooth brush, drawing paper, and tempera paints. Students will enjoy making spatter paintings by placing a leaf on the paper and brushing paint over the wire.

To help students understand how chlorophyll is manufactured in leaves, place a plant in the sunlight and cover one of the leaves. After three days remove the cover. This simple experiment will help the students to understand that sunlight is required to form chlorophyll.

Provide time for the students to draw a picture illustrating what autumn means to them. Display the pictures attractively.

Ask the students to collect products from nature to be added to an "Autumn Harvest" display for the school cafeteria or entrance hall. Pumpkins, gourds, nuts, Indian corn, acorns and autumn foliage may be combined to provide a brilliant splash of autumn beauty.

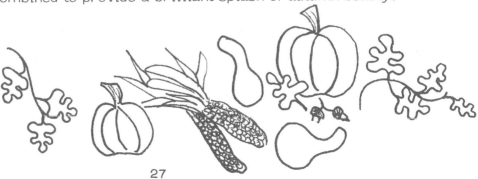

WOW
BOOK COVERS
ABOUT INDIAN
HEROES
MATH
WIGWAM WORRIES
10 X 3
2+2
28÷7
3/4+1/2
CLAY
1 cup flour
1 cup salt
+
water
Honoring the American Indian on September 28 opens doors to a proud heritage and a wonderous facet of American history.

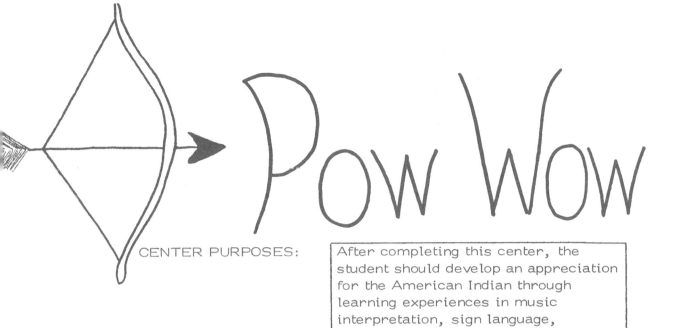

Pow Wow

CENTER PURPOSES:

> After completing this center, the student should develop an appreciation for the American Indian through learning experiences in music interpretation, sign language, observing life styles, and math computation.

CENTER ACTIVITIES:

Communications

"Smoke Signals"

Lead a small group discussion about the various signals Indians of yesterday used to communicate. These could include calls, drum beats, smoke signals, sign language, and pictograms. Instruct the students to work in pairs to develop their own special communications code. Once developed, they will enjoy sending each other messages to decode.

Creative Arts

"Chant Choice"

In a corner of the center, set up a listening station with a record player, head phones, and several records with Indian music. Instruct the students to select one chant to listen to, and with art supplies, draw the activity that is taking place during that particular chant.

When the pictures are displayed, a variety of Indian chores and activities will be shown.

Environmental Studies

"Diary Dilemma"

Provide art supplies for the students to use to make a small diary. Instruct them to record a day's activities in the diary. Then have them imagine they are an Indian boy and record their day's adventures as an Indian. Provide time for them to compare and contrast the life styles. Have them list the similarities and differences. Ask them to give reasons for the differences. Resource books may be provided to insure more accurate findings and results.

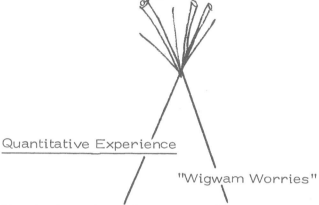

Quantitative Experience

"Wigwam Worries"

Use tagboard and tempera paint to make a small wigwam. Print addition, subtraction, multiplication and division problems on the strips of tagboard and put them inside the wigwam. Instruct the students to work in pairs to draw math problems from the wigwam and compete to find the most correct answers for the problems. New math problems may be added each day.

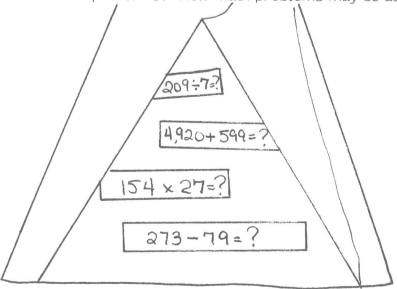

209 ÷ 7 = ?

4,920 + 599 = ?

154 × 27 = ?

273 − 79 = ?

"Bear Hunt"

Preparation Directions:

1. Enlarge the game board below on tagboard.
2. Using strips of tagboard, make twenty-five game cards with one, two, or three bear tracks on each. On four cards draw only a large question mark.
3. Provide three markers.

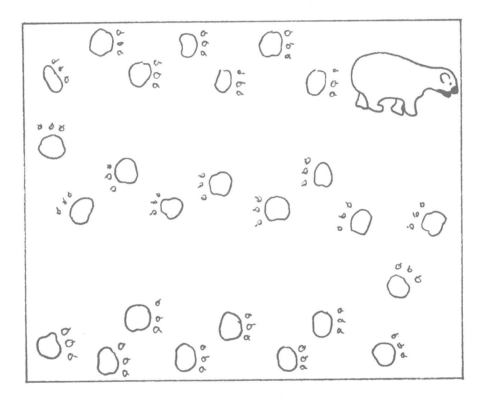

Player Directions:

1. Each player selects a marker and places it on the first track.
2. The cards are shuffled and placed face down.
3. Taking turns, players draw a card and move the number of spaces indicated. If a player draws a question mark, he loses his turn. (He's lost the trail.)
4. The first player to reach the bear wins the game!

JUST FOR FUN

Instruct the students to research a famous Indian, past or present, and make a report for the class. They may want to add interest by dressing like their "hero".

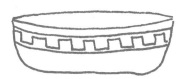

Provide a book of Indian folktales for the students to read. Some students may wish to tell the folktales to a small circle of classmates or to a younger group in another class.

Write to a reservation school and exchange letters with student pen pals, or write and exchange classroom letters.

Mix some clay to be used to make Indian pottery. After the pots have dried, provide tempera paints for the students to use to decorate their pots. By studying Indian art, some students may be able to paint authentic Indian designs.

A recipe for homemade clay:

1 cup flour, 1 cup salt, and enough water to make a very stiff dough.

Encourage the students to use resource books to discover different types of shelter once used by Indians. Provide art supplies for making models.

Instruct the students to imagine that they were Indians living a long time ago, and write a story using one of these ideas:

My first buffalo hunt   Spying on the enemy
A special message   A canoe trip
The medicine man's spell   When I grow up

DISPLAY REPORTS HERE
MAKE A MAP
MIX:
1 cup water +
1 cup salt
1 cup flour
Pencils
BOOKS
ABOUT
EXPLORATIONS
NINA
PINTA
SANTA MARIA

Ship Ashore
WRITE A NEWSPAPER ARTICLE
SAILORS' DELIGHT
US
"Pinta"
art stuff
....MAKE YOUR OWN BOAT......
GOOD NEWS!
The earth is not flat.
The vision of Christopher Columbus
continues to inspire people all over
the world to follow their dreams
to unknown destinations.

ship ashore

CENTER PURPOSES:

> After completing this center, the student should be familiar with Christopher Columbus and his activities through learning experiences in writing research reports, making relief maps, creative writing, and art.

CENTER ACTIVITIES:

Communications

"Action Reporters"

Instruct the students to pretend they are reporters for a large newspaper and have been given the following assignments:

Christopher Columbus is leaving today for a voyage. Interview Columbus and write a report for the newspaper.

You have been chosen to represent your newspaper and travel with Columbus to record the account of the voyage. Write a daily diary while you are on the trip.

Upon arriving in the new country, your assignment is to interview the people. Try to gather as much information as possible and write an article for the newspaper. You might want to include some pictures.

Prepare a map for the voyage home.

The voyage is over, and many people, including the Queen, are at the dock to greet Christopher Columbus. Write a detailed account of the welcoming festivities.

Creative Arts

"Sailors' Delight"

To stimulate student interest, read a story about Columbus and the Nina, the Pinta, and the Santa Maria. Lead a group discussion of the ships and how they are different from ships of today. Provide three large cardboard boxes, an old sheet, and art supplies to enable students to make the Nina, the Pinta, and the Santa Maria. Divide the class into three groups and ask each group to be responsible for one ship. After the ships are completed, place them in a quiet corner for the students to sit in while reading books about Columbus.

Environmental Studies

"Exploring the Unknown"

Place resource books in the center for the students to use to write a report comparing the voyage of Columbus and the first trip to the moon. Prepare an attractive bulletin board for displaying the reports.

Quantitative Experience

"Map Makers"

Provide poster board, flour, salt, and art supplies to enable the students to make a relief map of Columbus' voyage*. Instruct the students to include on the map North America, Bahama Islands, Cuba, Haiti, Spain, Africa, and the Atlantic Ocean. Ask the students to develop the route taken by the Nina, Pinta, and the Santa Maria, and to include a legend on the map.

*Use the following recipe:

    1 cup flour
    1 cup salt
    Enough water to make a stiff dough

"Stay on Course"

Preparation Directions:

1. Enlarge the game board below on tagboard.

2. Using tagboard, make fourteen player cards with the following ideas:

    storm blowing...lose one turn
    hoist the sail...move one space
    all hands on deck...get an extra turn
    land sighted...move ahead two spaces
    swab the decks...go back one space
    polish the brass...move one space
    chow time...get an extra turn
    orders from the captain...move ahead two spaces
    man the lifeboats...move one space
    inspection day...loose one turn
    repair the sails...move ahead two spaces
    caught a fish...move one space
    seasick...lose one turn
    stand watch...move ahead two spaces

3. Provide three ship markers.

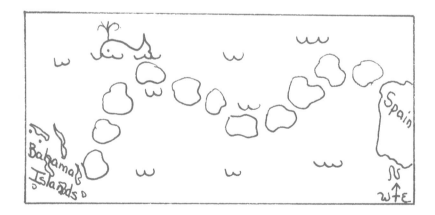

Player Directions:

1. Each player selects a marker and places it on Spain.

2. The cards are shuffled and placed face down.

3. Taking turns, players draw a card and move the number of spaces indicated.

4. The first player to reach the Bahama Islands wins the game.

JUST FOR FUN

Provide construction paper, magic markers and scissors for the students to use to create Columbus' Coat of Arms.

Columbus persuaded the Queen of Spain to provide support for ships and money for his voyage. Instruct the students to think of an adventure they would like to take, and present their plan in the form of a creative story to the President of the United States for his support.

Using the music of a well known song, the students might enjoy writing words that the sailors might have sung on Columbus' voyage.

The sea is stormy...

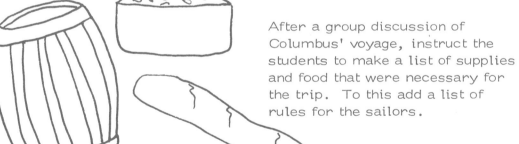

After a group discussion of Columbus' voyage, instruct the students to make a list of supplies and food that were necessary for the trip. To this add a list of rules for the sailors.

Design two games for the sailors on the Nina, the Pinta, and the Santa Maria to play to pass the time away while at sea.

HALLOWEEN

MAKE YOUR OWN COSTUME

TRICK OR TREAT

BAGS

art

BOX OF 1¢ CANDY

BOOKS

Everyone looks forward to October 31 when ghosts, witches, and goblins rule the day.

CENTER PURPOSES:

After completing this center, the student should develop understanding and appreciation for Halloween through learning experiences in costume design, pantomime, plant growth and the use of geometric shapes.

CENTER ACTIVITIES:

Communications

"Trick or Treat"

Make a trick or treat sack containing wrapped Halloween candy. On each piece of candy attach the name of a character associated with Halloween (ghost, bat, witch, or cat). Direct a small group of students to draw a "treat". Before they eat it, they must pantomime the character, while the other students work in groups to try to identify it. The group guessing correctly gets the next "turn". Many students will enjoy adding their own characters to the list to be identified.

Creative Arts

"Bag It"

Provide large grocery bags and art supplies; invite the students to create their own Halloween costumes. Instruct them to cut a neck opening in the bottom of the bag, and armholes in the sides. They will enjoy decorating smaller bags or paper plates (with an elastic band) for their face masks for the Halloween party. Prizes may be awarded for the most original, the scariest, the prettiest, and the ugliest costumes.

Environmental Studies

"Pumpkin Parade"

Provide resource books to enable students to trace the growth of a pumpkin from seed to harvest. Some students may wish to plant some seeds and observe and record daily or weekly changes. Using the resource books, the students may list the uses of a pumpkin, then in small groups demonstrate activities such as baking a pie, cake or bread, or drying and salting pumpkin seeds.

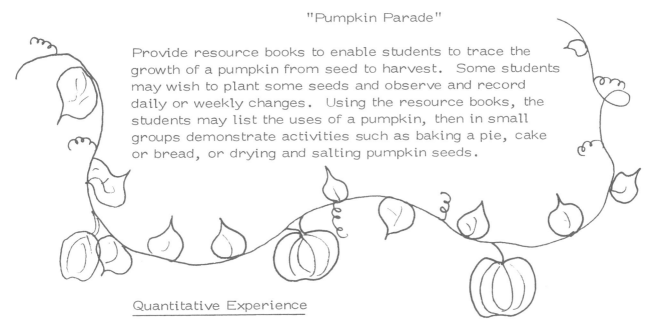

Quantitative Experience

"Scary Scene"

Instruct the students to make a "spooky scene" using only rectangles, squares, triangles, and circles cut from construction paper. Once the scene is completed the scary scenes may be exchanged to allow other students to locate the shapes found in the "spooky scenes". A prize could be awarded to the student including the most shapes in his completed project.

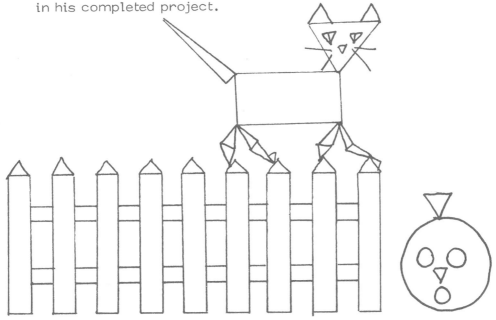

"Ghost Getaway"

"Let me out!" Stay on the lines until you find the back door.

44

JUST FOR FUN

Have the students tear construction paper (no scissors allowed) to make a "mod" jack-o-lantern, witch or black cat.

Let the students write spooky, scary stories or poems. Mount each one on a Halloween shape cut from construction paper.

Use a plastic jack-o-lantern as the container to hold tagboard strips on which the following words have been printed:

corn field	ghost
haunted house	children
cemetery	pumpkin
street	broom
moon	trick or treating
scarecrow	cat
witch	scream

Instruct the students to draw three words to include in a Halloween story.

Interested students may wish to write a Halloween play. Arrange for them to pantomime the story behind a sheet in a darkened room while eerie music is played in the background.

Make paper bag pumpkins! Supply brown lunch bags and instruct students to crinkle newspaper and stuff the bag. Twist the top two inches of the bag to form the handle. Paint the pumpkin orange and use black paint to make a face.

CENTER PURPOSES:

> After completing this center, the student should develop understanding and appreciation for Halloween through learning experiences in art, writing riddles, using the five senses, and problem solving.

CENTER ACTIVITIES:

Communications

"Boo! Guess Who!"

Instruct students to write a riddle about something they might see in a haunted house. Create a mood by lighting a candle or a jack-o-lantern in a darkened room. Read the riddles one at a time and see if the students can guess what is in the haunted house.

Creative Arts

"Dreadful Dioramas"

Read or tell a story about a haunted house.

Using shoe boxes and art supplies, ask the students to work as couples to create a spooky room for the haunted house. Stack and attach the dioramas to form a house. The students might then enjoy creating new open-ended stories about the family that lived in the haunted house.

Environmental Studies

"Silly Senses"

Set the stage for the students to test their five senses in the haunted house. Instruct them to think of one thing they might see in the haunted house. Have them use the first letter of whatever they might see as the first letter of each thing they will taste, hear, feel and smell.

Example: see a spider, taste a sprinkle of
sawdust, hear a scream, feel a
skeleton, and smell snake stew

Quantitative Experience

"Enter and Escape"

Use tagboard and art supplies to make a haunted house. Cut out the windows and doors and mount the house on the bulletin board. In each window, copy one of the following problems:

1. Wilma Witch is stirring her famous brew. She needs twenty-two bat wings. How many bats must she catch?

2. The recipe calls for nineteen toad stools. She must triple the recipe. How many must she pick?

3. Sixty, or two-thirds, of the witches are coming to Wilma's party. How many witches did she invite?

4. She has only fifty-seven broom spaces. How many more does she need for her guests?

5. How many witches will there be in each room if there are fifteen rooms?

When every problem is solved correctly, the student escapes the Haunted House.

"Witches' Hideout"

Preparation Directions:

1. Enlarge the game board below on tagboard.

2. Each space on the board has a circle of red, green or purple. Some spaces have an object on them.

3. Make thirty-five tagboard cards. Ten cards should have red circles, ten purple circles and ten green circles. One card should have a picture of a broom, one a witch, one a ghost, one a black cat and one a bat.

4. Make jack-o-lantern markers for each player.

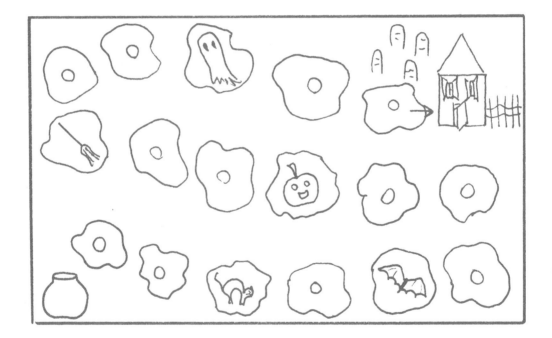

Player Directions:

1. Place players' markers in the pot.

2. Shuffle the cards and place face down.

3. Taking turns, players draw cards and move to the space indicated on the card.

4. The first player to reach the "Witches' Hideout" wins the game.

JUST FOR FUN

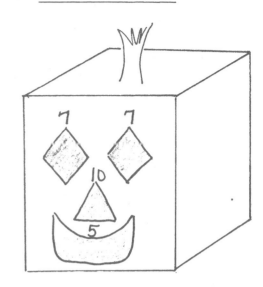

Using a large (3' x 3') heavy cardboard box cut a jack-o-lantern face in one end. Label the mouth five points, the eyes seven points, and the nose ten points. Provide a bean bag and let students divide into teams. The first side to score seventy points wins!

Instruct students to pretend they are friendly ghosts who need a new home. Provide time for them to write about their "ghostly" adventures.

Provide orange and black construction paper for the students to use to make pumpkins with faces and accordian arms and legs. Display the pumpkin creatures on a white picket fence made from construction paper.

Provide large paper doll shapes (two feet) cut from butcher paper, yarn, feathers, construction paper, and other scrap materials. Ask each student to "costume" his paper doll as he would like to dress on Halloween.

Sound the Alarm

WRITE A LETTER

BUCKET BRIGADE

Lives and property can be saved through the study of fire prevention.

CENTER PURPOSES:

After completing this center, the
student should develop awareness
of fire prevention through learning
experiences in researching the
history of fire, writing a class
newspaper, and fire hazards.

CENTER ACTIVITIES:

Communications

"Hot Line"

To develop student awareness of fire prevention techniques,
plan and write a class newspaper to be taken home.   The
newspaper might contain articles about the following ideas:

Fire drills at school   Safeguards in public buildings
Turning in the alarm   for preventing fires
Camping and campfires   Fire hazards in homes
Fire Prevention Week   First Aid
Fireproofing materials   Firemen

Comics and crossword puzzles might also be included in the
newspaper.

Creative Arts

"Bucket Brigade"

To help students become familiar with the history of fire
fighting, place resource books in the center. Encourage
small group discussions for sharing the newly acquired
information about fire fighting. Provide art supplies to
enable the students to paint a mural showing the various ways
people have fought fires, from using the bucket brigade to
the most modern fire engines and equipment.

Environmental Studies

"What's It All About?"

Take a field trip to the fire station nearest the school. Plan
the trip carefully with the person in charge of the fire station
so that the equipment and its use, the life style of firemen,
and other aspects of the fire department's contribution to
society are presented. If a field trip is not possible, invite
a fireman to come to the classroom to serve as a resource
person.

As a follow-up activity, the students will enjoy writing letters
of appreciation to the firemen.

Quantitative Experience

"Fire Hazards"

Place drawing paper, crayons, and rulers in the center.
Instruct the students to draw an inside view of a house, six
inches tall and seven inches wide with a one-inch roof. The
house should have three floors with the following rooms and
dimensions:

Basement – two rooms, each three and one-half
inches wide and two inches tall

First Floor – living room and kitchen, each two and
one-half inches wide and two inches tall;
den, two inches wide and two inches tall

Second Floor – two bedrooms, each three inches wide
and two inches tall; bathroom, one inch
wide and two inches tall

Ask the students to draw pictures inside each room showing fire
hazards found in homes. The back of the picture may be used
to list ways to prevent these fires from taking place.

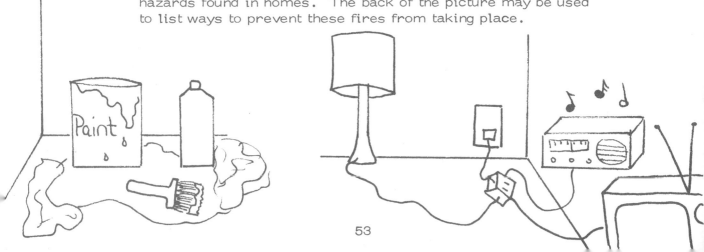

"Screeching Sirens"

Preparation Directions:

1. Enlarge the game board on tagboard.

2. Write the following directions on strips of tagboard:

> What is a good way to put out a campfire?
> How should one put out a lighted cigarette?
> How would you report a fire?
> Give one good rule to follow in a fire drill.
> Why is it important to close all windows and doors
>   if there is a fire?
> Why do we have Fire Prevention Week?
> If your clothes are on fire, what is the best thing to do?
> Why is it dangerous to smoke in bed?
> Tell one fire hazard that can be found in homes?
> Give one fire prevention slogan.
> Give one way you can help prevent fires.
> (Other questions may be added.)

3. Provide three fire engine markers.

Player Directions:

1. Each player selects a marker and places it on "Start".

2. The cards are shuffled and placed face down. Taking
   turns players draw a card, answer the question and move
   one space. If they cannot answer the question, they cannot move.

3. The first player to reach the "Fire Station" wins the game.

JUST FOR FUN

Provide art supplies for the students to make posters and write slogans for "Fire Prevention Week".

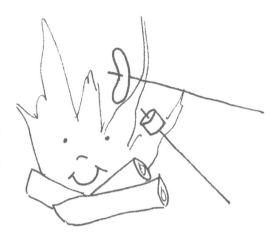

Divide the class into two groups. At a given signal, one group will make a list of things showing how fire can be a friend, and one group will make a list of things showing how fire can be an enemy.

At the end of fifteen minutes share the lists and compare them.

The students might enjoy writing "Fire Prevention" jingles and taping them to share with another class.

Divide the class into small groups to write "Fire Prevention" plays to be presented to the class.

Tour the school building and grounds to locate fire hazards.

Write a creative story from one of the following ideas:

I was walking through the forest and met Smokey the Bear...

The fireman gasped! His hose had run out of water...

The careless campers forgot to put me out...

I was toasting a marshmallow and...

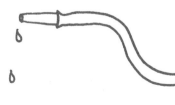

Platform Writer
Republican
Vot
Hit the Trail—
Plan a campaign and make a map...
campaign trail
vote for me

CENTER PURPOSES:

> After completing this center, the
> student should develop interest and
> enthusiasm for an election through
> learning experiences in writing
> jingles, slogans or songs, creating
> campaign hats and buttons, developing
> a campaign platform, and mapping a
> campaign route.

CENTER ACTIVITIES:

Communications

"Vote Getters"

For national, state, city, school or classroom elections, jingles,
slogans, and songs are usually written. Ask the students to
write a jingle, slogan, or song for a candidate running for an
office. The students will enjoy presenting a television program
to the class or another class where their jingle, slogan or song
may be heard.

Or...

"Chore-a-thon"

Using the idea of a telethon, select four students to act as hosts
for a television program. Divide the class into two groups to
represent two candidates. The hosts of the TV program will then
accept from the students any of the following ideas to help their
candidate win:

1. Carry books for the candidate
2. Clean the candidate's desk
3. Shine the candidate's shoes
4. Hang up the candidate's coat
5. Make campaign posters

Creative Arts

"Campaign Gimmicks"

Provide art supplies for the students to create a campaign hat. A prize may be awarded for the most creative hat. Campaign buttons may also be made to accompany the hats.

Environmental Studies

"Platform Writers"

Lead a group discussion on the importance of a candidate having a "platform" during a campaign. Ask the students to read the papers to obtain different views of candidates running for office. As a class activity let the students collectively write a "platform" for a class president. Then instruct the students to select an office to which they would like to be elected and write a "platform". Provide time for sharing of the "platforms".

Quantitative Experience

"Hit the Trail"

Every candidate must spend a certain amount of time visiting the voters to try to win votes. Instruct the students to plan one campaign trip. This can be in the school, in the neighborhood, in their city, or to a neighboring city or state. A daily schedule of appearances must be included. Provide art materials and rulers for the students to draw a map of their trip. The map must include a legend showing the distances on the trip. Ask the students to share their maps and compute the number of miles traveled by each candidate.

"Puzzle Power"

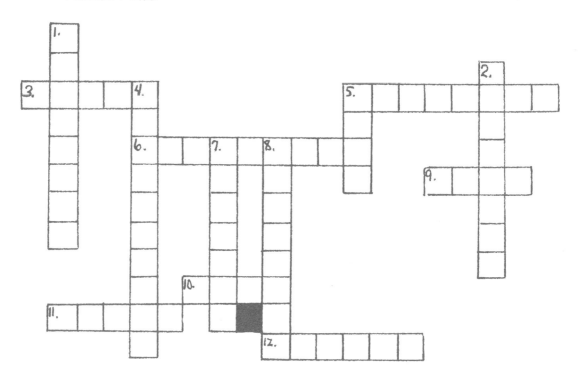

Across

3. Highest elected official in a city.

5. Every candidate must do this to win.

6. Highest elected official in the United States.

9. It is everyone's duty to ____.

10. A president of the United States is elected every ___ years.

11. A candidate must ___ to many groups.

12. A candidate running for the office of president must be at least ____ years of age.

Down

1. A candidate's ideas or what he wants to accomplish is called a _____.

2. A person must be _____ years of age to vote.

4. and 8. Two political parties in the United States.

5. A major is an elected official in every _____.

7. Two of these are elected from each state.

JUST FOR FUN

The students will enjoy designing
bumper stickers supporting their
favorite candidate to place on
their desks.

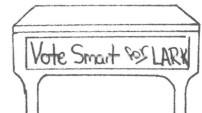

Invite different candidates
currently running for local
offices to speak to the
students.

Provide art supplies for the
students to make election
posters to place in the room
or in the school hallway.

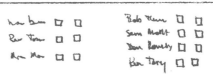

Visit a voting precinct so
the students can see a voting
machine. Secure a large box
for the class to use to prepare
their own voting machine.
Provide time for the students
to vote for their favorite
candidate.

Ask the students to use one of the
following ideas to write an imaginary story:

    The Case of the Missing Ballots
    I dreamed that I was elected to...
    I needed one more vote, so I...
    Making an important campaign speech, I suddenly
      lost my voice and...

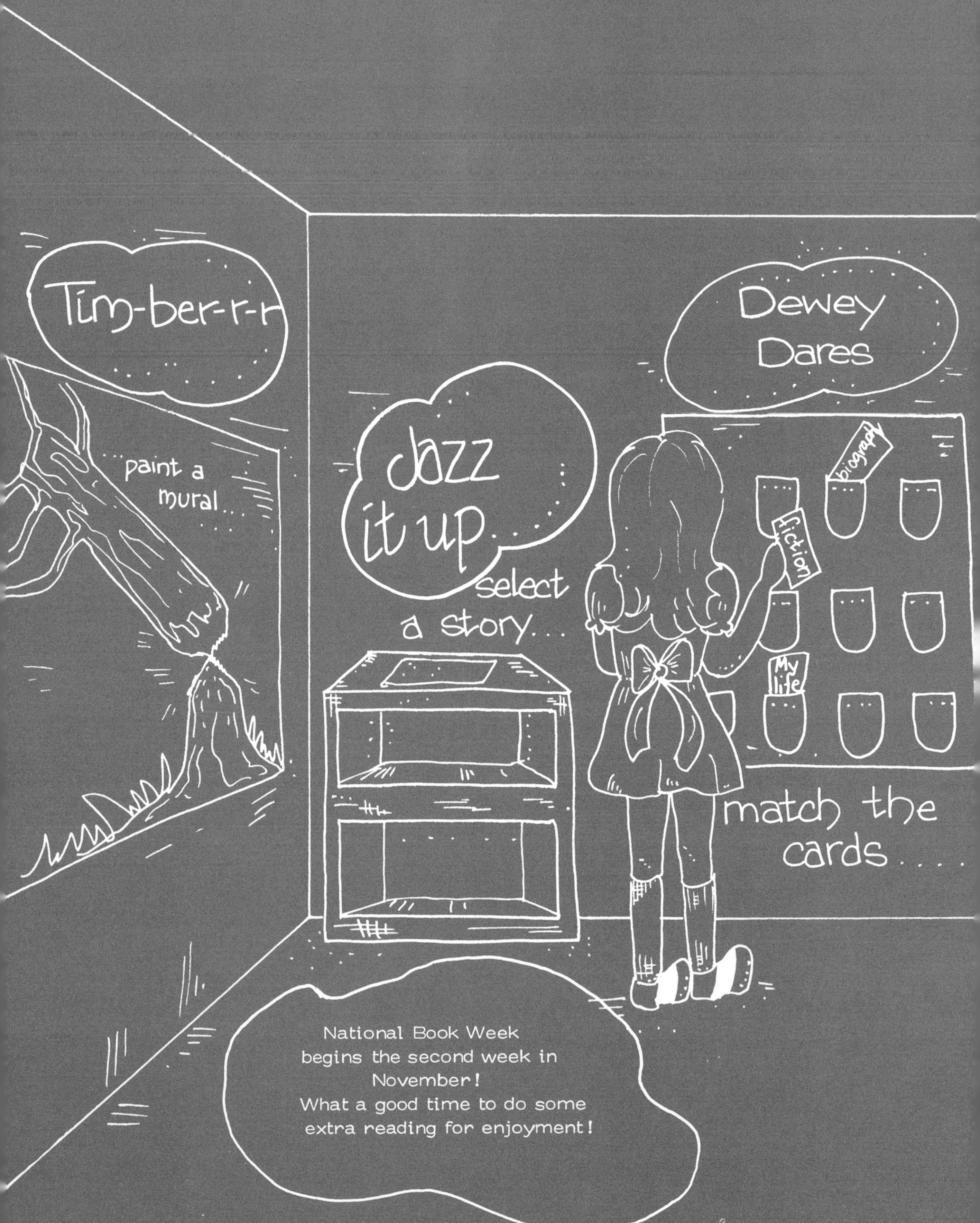
Tim-ber-r-r
paint a mural...
Dewey Dares
dazz it up...
select a story...
biography
fiction
My life
match the cards....
National Book Week begins the second week in November! What a good time to do some extra reading for enjoyment!

Read

Play
Day

present a
story by

... using scarves
... making puppets
... paint a mural
... create a TV show
... being original

In a
Bind

mural paper

CENTER PURPOSES:

> After completing this center, the student should develop appreciation for books through learning experiences in book illustration, play production, paper making, and the use of the Dewey Decimal System.

CENTER ACTIVITIES:

Communications

"Play Day"

Divide the students into small groups to select a favorite book to be shared with the rest of the class in a special way. A chart placed in the center might carry the following suggestions:

Tell your story by:

...using the box of scarves to plan and present a song and dance review

...making and using paper—sack puppets and a theater constructed from the cardboard box holding the sacks, glue, scissors, colored paper, yarn and buttons

...selecting your own materials from the art table to use to paint a mural

...writing and presenting a television program

...using a creative idea of your own

Creative Arts

"Jazz It Up"

Select ten picture books and copy each story separately.
Place the ten stories in the center and ask the students to
select a story to illustrate using the art materials supplied
in the center. The students will enjoy comparing their
versions to the original picture books.

Environmental Studies

"TIM – Ber–r–r!"

Provide encyclopedias and resource books for the students
to use to trace the use of wood in paper production. In a
corner, place mural paper so that this process can be
drawn from start to finish as the students learn the
sequence of the process. Provide space in the center to
display the mural.

Quantitative Experience

"Dewey Dares!"

Make a chart for the center including the categories from
the Dewey Decimal System. Make a concentration game
by gluing twenty–four card pockets on a sheet of tagboard.
In each pocket, place a 3 x 5 index card. On twelve cards
write the different Dewey Decimal categories. On the
twelve other cards, write the title of books that would
match the categories. Taking turns, let the students try
to match the book with the category. The student making
the most matches will be the winner of the game.

"All Parts Accounted For!"

Across:

1. Person or company who offers books for sale.

3. Person who writes a book.

4. Name of a book.

5. An extra section at the end of a book.

7. The exclusive right to copy a book is a _____ .

10. The _____ of contents lists the pages of each section of a book.

Down:

2. Person who draws the pictures in a book.

6. Alphabetical list of items in book.

8. These make up a book.

9. Section of a book.

JUST FOR FUN

Provide time for a book swap.
Let students bring a book from
home that they would like to
exchange. Display the books and
then provide time for the big swap.

Help the class to select a well-known author and provide time
for everyone to read one of his books. (Dr. Seuss, Marguerite
Henry, Laura Ingalls Wilder, Beverly Cleary, Ezra Keats,
E. B. White) Lead a discussion of the author's style.

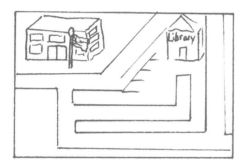

Discuss with the students the
location of the closest library.
Ask them for help in drawing a
map of the route from the school
to the library. Provide art
supplies for the students to use
in making maps of the route from
their homes to the library.

Take a field trip to a book bindery, a printing company, or the
community library.

Instruct the students to write a story to be made into a book.
Provide art supplies for illustrating the stories and set up an
assembly line for a book bindery. Ask the students to sign up
for one of the following stations:

1. Inspect the order of the book, and add an extra sheet to
    front and back.
2. Using needles and thread, sew the book together.
3. Cut two cardboard pages the exact size of the book pages.
4. Cut fabric one inch longer than the open book and drymount
    with an iron to the cardboard.
5. Drymount with an iron to insert the book in its cover.
6. Fold the edges of the fabric to finish the edges of the cover.

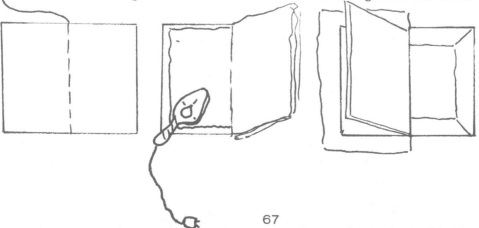

Beginner
Barters

Barter
Box

Big
Builders

Tu

T

Since 1623 Americans
have set aside time to give
thanks for the blessings the year
has brought. Feasting and visiting
are the order of
the day.

CENTER PURPOSES:

After completing this center, the student should develop understanding of and appreciation for Thanksgiving through learning experiences in writing a script and presenting a puppet show, making a recipe book, building an Indian or Pilgrim village, and practicing bartering.

CENTER ACTIVITIES:

Communications

"Yum Yum"

Provide resource books to enable the students to plan a Thanksgiving menu similar to the one served by the Pilgrims and Indians on the first Thanksgiving. Help the students to locate recipes for all the above dishes and make a cookbook containing the recipes. Ask the students to illustrate the recipes and make colorful covers. Allow the class to select one of the recipes to prepare in the classroom for everyone to enjoy.

Creative Arts

"The Big Show"

Instruct the students to write a script for a Thanksgiving puppet show that involves two characters. Explain that the script can be about an early Thanksgiving or a modern Thanksgiving and the characters may be people or animals. Provide the necessary art materials to enable the students to make sock puppets. Allow time for a puppet show to be presented in an audience situation.

Environmental Studies

"Big Builders"

Provide resource books to enable the students to research
Indian and Pilgrim villages. Divide the class into two
groups. Instruct one group to make an Indian village and
one group to make a Pilgrim village. Provide the cardboard boxes and the necessary art materials for the students
to use to complete the project. Display the villages in
the school entrance hall, cafeteria or library for students
in other classes to enjoy.

Quantitative Experience

"Beginner Barters"

The Indians and Pilgrims practiced bartering. Lead a
group discussion to enable the students to understand
bartering. Plan a day when they can bring an object from
home that they wish to barter. Provide a corner of the
room for displaying and bartering for the items.

"Turkey Chase"

Preparation Directions:

1. Enlarge the game board below on tagboard.

2. On strips of tagboard write the following ideas:

    Someone said turkeys were hiding in the trees. Go look!
    Caught in tall grass. Move to it.
    Found tracks. Follow them. Oops, not turkey!
    You're caught in the rain...lose turkey.
    Must cross water. Can turkeys swim?
    You hear a gobble. Move two spaces.
    Ask the rabbit for a clue.
    I've spotted something...no turkey! Move three spaces.
    Stop at the house...ask the farmer.
    It's getting late. Move one space.
    Take a break and eat...move two spaces.
    I think I'm being tricked. Move three spaces.

3. Provide three markers.

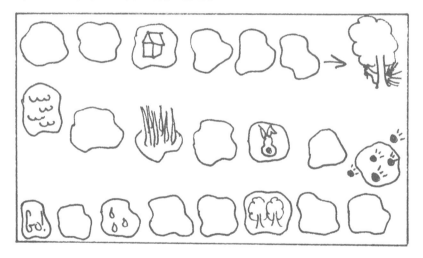

Player Directions:

1. Each player selects a marker and places it on the board.

2. The cards are shuffled and placed in a stack face down.

3. Taking turns, players draw a card and move according to
    the directions. The first player to reach the turkey wins
    the chase!

JUST FOR FUN

Provide various sizes and shapes of
noodles and dry cereals to enable the
students to make a turkey mosaic.
Cornshucks for feathers and corn
for eyes, nose, and mouth may be
used. A variety of seeds could also
be used for this activity.

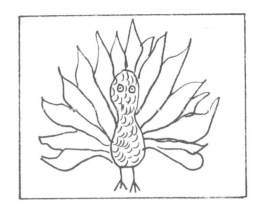

Ask one-half of the students to
make a list of ten things for which
they are thankful. Ask the remaining
students to make a list of ten things
for which the Pilgrims were thankful.
Provide time for comparing the list.

Instruct the students to write
a "pretending" story using one
of the following ideas:

Pretend you are a turkey. How will you escape being served
for a Thanksgiving dinner?

Pretend you have visited a turkey farm. Write the conversation
that takes place between two turkeys just before Thanksgiving.

Ask the students to select an
Indian group to research and
use as the subject of an oral
report. Costumes may be
made to wear while giving the
reports.

Provide art supplies for the
students to make a cornucopia.
Paper mache vegetables and
fruits may be added.

73

Br-r-r
Deep
Freeze

wintry
Wonder-
land

weather
Station

COLD
WAVE

M T W T F S S

Br-r-r-r, it's cold
outside, and the first day
of Winter is the perfect
time for fun and games.

arrange strips to form snowflake

slushy

soggy

billowy

snowflake structure

snowflake swirl

POPCORN

CENTER PURPOSES:

After completing this center, the student should develop under-standing and appreciation for the beginning of winter through learning experiences in art, using descriptive words, winter activities, and weather forecasting.

CENTER ACTIVITIES:

Communications

"Snowflake Structure"

Assist the students in listing words that describe snow. Ask them to use white construction paper as a background on which to arrange the descriptive words to form a snowflake shape. The snowflakes may later be cut out and displayed in the center.

Creative Arts

"Snowflake Swirl"

Provide art supplies for the students to use to make snow scenes featuring popcorn, soap flakes mixed with water to fingerpaint consistency, and spray snow or white chalk on a background of black construction paper. On a bulletin board mount the completed creations.

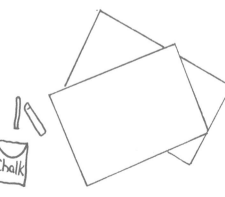

Environmental Studies

"Wintry Wonderland"

Prepare a bulletin board in the shape of a house. Upstairs draw a boy in bed, downstairs draw mother in the kitchen, and draw father working in the basement. Draw a girl outside. Ask the students to draw, cut out, and mount in the correct part of the house:

1. An outfit the boy will need for winter

2. Food the family will prepare during the winter

3. A job that must be done to get the house ready for winter

4. An outside winter fun activity for the girl or for the boy

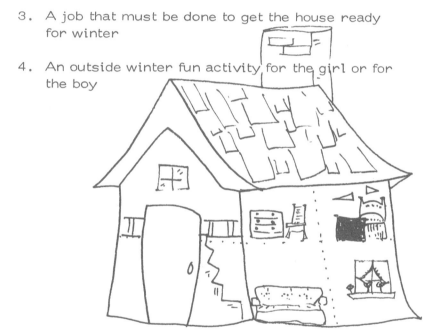

Quantitative Experience

"Cold Wave"

Make daily weather maps and temperature charts available. Instruct the students to select a city and for five days record its temperatures and the temperatures of their city. Ask them to compare the results and suggest what conditions the recorded temperatures might bring about.

"Whiz Through Winter"

Circle any words that remind you of winter. The words are
written diagonally, horizontally and vertically.

D	D	E	C	E	M	B	E	R	A	D	G
E	S	C	H	R	I	S	T	M	A	S	H
B	L	I	Z	Z	A	R	D	B	W	S	E
F	E	S	N	O	W	M	O	B	I	L	E
G	D	I	G	L	O	O	F	C	N	E	H
I	D	H	J	K	N	J	R	F	T	I	I
M	I	T	T	E	N	S	E	M	E	G	B
Q	N	S	H	O	C	K	E	Y	R	H	E
R	G	S	K	L	M	O	Z	P	L	R	R
V	T	U	K	I	S	L	E	E	T	I	N
Z	W	X	I	C	I	C	L	E	S	D	A
B	Y	X	Y	S	A	N	T	A	N	E	T
O	S	K	A	T	I	N	G	S	O	N	I
O	V	E	R	C	O	A	T	N	W	P	O
T	Z	E	R	O	Z	A	R	O	B	Q	N
S	B	D	C	L	T	M	N	W	A	S	U
S	L	P	R	D	R	M	P	O	L	V	T
T	S	N	O	W	M	A	N	X	L	W	R

JUST FOR FUN

During or immediately after the first
snowstorm, provide time for students
to write poetry. Instruct them to write
an icicle poem or snowball poem,
writing until the lines in the poem have
formed that shape. (If there is no
snowstorm, create the environment
for this activity by reading poetry and
stories, or by viewing a film or filmstrip.)

Icicles Hang
Very Heavy
Dripping
Drips
Until
All
G
O
N
E

Winter is:

Cover a bulletin board with
sky blue paper. Mount a
thick layer of cotton batting
at the bottom, and label the
board

"Winter is..."

Provide art supplies for the
students to draw, cut out,
and mount winter pictures.

Provide white paper and scissors to enable the students to fold
squares of paper to be cut into snowflakes. On a bulletin board
mount all the snowflakes to form a snowman. Eyes, nose and
mouth may be added with crayons or magic markers.

Ask the students to write a story: "What would I say to a talking
snowman?"

Make resource books available for
students to use to study the winter
habits of a chosen animal.

Provide magazines and art supplies for the students to use to
produce a collage depicting a winter scene.

The Feast of Lights is one of the happiest and most anticipated Jewish holidays. It is a time of thanksgiving and gift giving.

CENTER PURPOSES:

> After completing this center, the student should develop appreciation of Hanukkah through learning experiences in writing creative stories, reading resource books, listening to a rabbi, making a circle game and designing gift wrapping paper.

CENTER ACTIVITIES:

Communications

"Pic A Word"

During Hanukkah gifts are exchanged and children anxiously await each night so they can open their gifts. Prepare one attractively covered box. Print the following words on cards; place the cards in the box and wrap the box as a gift.

holiday	package	eight days	ribbon	grandparents
gifts	oil	doll	dreidel	children
toy	candle	watch	candy	menorah

Instruct the students to open the gift box, draw a card, and use that word in a sentence to begin a creative story. Continue to draw a word and write a sentence until all the words have been used and the story is completed. Provide time for the students to share their stories.

Creative Arts

"Print Out"

Provide a collection of small boxes, tempera paint, white shelf paper, dull knives, and potatoes. Give each student one half of a potato and let them cut a design. Using the potato, tempera paint, and shelf paper, ask the students to design their own Hanukkah gift wrapping paper. The gift wrapping paper may be used to cover the small boxes or taken home to wrap a Hanukkah gift.

Environmental Studies

"Candle Glow"

Place resource books in the center and instruct the students to read about Hanukkah. Let each student write one question on Hanukkah. Invite a rabbi or other resource person to visit the class. Encourage the students to submit their questions to the visitor to enable them to learn more about Hanukkah. Provide a menorah and candles and light one additional candle each day.

Quantitative Experience

"Dreidel Spinners"

Demonstrate making a circle by using a compass, string and a pencil. Explain and illustrate the meaning of diameter, radius, and circumference. Instruct the students to make various sized circles and measure the diameter and radius of each circle. The students will enjoy making their own game. Instruct two students to work together to draw a large circle, either on the floor or on a large piece of drawing paper; mark the center point of the circle. Provide a dreidel for the students to spin. Instruct them to place the dreidel on the center point and take turns spinning it. The player whose dreidel lands closest to the center point of the circle gets one point. The player who gets ten points first "wins" the game.

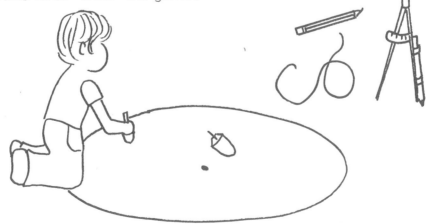

"Gift Game"

Preparation Directions:

1. Enlarge the game board below on tagboard.

2. Prepare two lists of spelling words and print each list on a separate card. The spelling words may be related to Hanukkah.

3. Provide two markers.

Player Directions:

1. Each player takes a card with a list of words on it.

2. Taking turns, players give words to each other. If the word is spelled correctly, the player places his marker on the first gift. If he does not spell the word correctly, he cannot move.

3. The first person to open all the gifts wins the game.

JUST FOR FUN

Prepare a bulletin board and provide
colored construction paper and paste
for the students to use to make a mosaic
menorah.

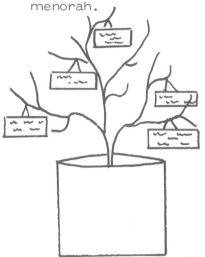

Using a tree branch, make a
riddle tree. Ask the students
to write a Hanukkah riddle and
hang it on the tree for their
classmates to guess. An example
could be:

It shines every night
to cast a glow so bright?

I spin and turn and when I land
you take a piece from the candy pan?

Instruct the students to use one
of the following words as the theme of a
poem:

dreidel
candle
holiday
menorah

Play a "Gift Guessing Game". One
student thinks of a Hanukkah gift and
gives three clues. The first person
to guess the gift wins, and he becomes
the leader. Continue to play until
each student in the group has a chance
to give gift clues.

Take a field trip to a synagogue or temple.

Santa's
Tasty Trimmings
ham
79¢
milk
58¢
lettuce
92¢
BOOKS ON CUSTOMS
STOCKING STUFFERS
Merry Christmas
TOTAL COST OF STOCKING STUFFERS

spree

DESIGN
SANTA'S
SUIT

PLACE
NOUNS ON
CANDY CANES

ornament
tree
snowflake

Toyland
Tizzy

The excitement and
anticipation associated
with the pre-Christmas
season provides special
motivation in itself for
sparkling classroom
dynamics.

CENTER PURPOSES:

> After completing this center, the student should develop an appreciation for Christmas through learning experiences in art, studying Christmas customs in other lands, and problem solving.

CENTER ACTIVITIES:

Communications

"Santa's Shopping List"

Challenge the students to write a sentence about Santa by beginning each word in the sentence with a letter from this activity's title. They must use the letters in the consecutive order.

Example: Santa and Nancy Thomas are sending Santa's helper over Paris...

Creative Arts

"Santa's Style Show"

Draw a large Santa poster showing Santa wearing only underwear. Print the following instructions on the poster.

"Santa's suit is worn out. Design a new one. See how creative you can be."

Provide art supplies for the students to use to portray their wildest imaginations concerning a wardrobe for Santa.

Environmental Studies

"Customs Kaleidoscope"

Provide resource books for the students to use to discover
Christmas customs in other countries. Instruct them to find
a game, activity or song to teach to the class. A special
part of each day might be set aside for learning about and
sharing a new Christmas custom.

Mexico

Quantitative Experience

"Tasty Trimmings"

On a bulletin board in the center mount the grocery ads from
a current newspaper. Instruct the students to plan their Christmas
dinner and to compute the total cost of their dinner. Ask them
to keep in mind the number of people to be served, the quantity
of each item to be purchased and the necessity of figuring prices
by the pound, gallon, etc.

"Rudolph's Route"

Help Rudolph find his way through the storm, to your chimney.

JUST FOR FUN

Create your own workshop and encourage the students to make
gifts for their parents.

Make fudge with an electric skillet, wooden
spoon and this recipe:

4 c. sugar   Cook over medium heat
1 c. evaporated milk   to soft ball stage.
1 c. butter

Remove from heat and add 12 oz. package chocolate
chips, one pint marshmellow creme, and one tsp.
vanilla. Beat until chocolate melts. Pour into a
buttered 13" x 9" x 2" pan.

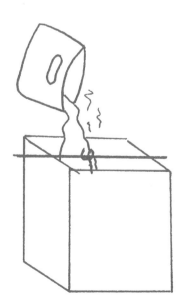

Purchase cotton finger tip towels
for the students to use red or green
waterproof paints to "handprint"
their towels.

Make fancy Christmas candles! Use
milk cartons for the mold, and paraffin
and red or green crayons for the candles.
Melt the paraffin and crayons carefully.
Tie the candle wick to a stick resting on
the top of the carton. Fill the carton with
melted paraffin; let it harden; peel the
carton off--and presto, you have a
Christmas candle fit to light any holiday
dinner table.

CENTER PURPOSES:

After completing this center, the student should develop appreciation for Christmas through learning experiences in art, using descriptive words, constructing bird feeders, and problem solving.

CENTER ACTIVITIES:

Communications

"Candy Canes"

Cut candy cane shapes from tagboard and print a Christmas noun on each candy cane:

sleigh	tree	snowflake
ornament	stocking	Santa
present	star	

Hang each candy cane on a small artificial tree. Place the tree in the center. Ask the students to select a noun and use descriptive words to create colorful phrases.

Creative Arts

"Toyland Tizzy"

Fill a brightly covered cardboard box with the following supplies:

toothpicks	ribbon	buttons
small boxes	yarn	styrofoam
tempera paint	fabric scraps	foil
glitter	pins	cardboard tubes

Instruct the students to use the art supplies to create a toy for Santa's workshop. The toys may be displayed on a classroom shelf.

Environmental Studies

"Tempting Trees"

The students will enjoy making bird feeders to hang on trees near the school. Provide empty milk cartons with a square opening cut in two sides about one inch from the bottom of the carton. Instruct the students to cover the outside of the carton with contact paper, popsicle sticks, twigs, or dull foil, and run heavy string or wire through the top of the carton so the feeder can be hung from a tree branch. Seed or suet can be put in the bottom of the new feeder. (Your next center activity might be bird watching!)

Quantitative Experience

"Stocking Stuffers"

Make a large felt stocking and fill it with small toys (car, whistle, ball and jacks, candy cane, plastic orange, bag of marbles, rubber insect, toothbrush, yo-yo, squirt gun). Use small squares of tape to label the price on each toy. Instruct the students to total the cost of the "Stocking Stuffers". (Keeping the candy cane for a treat will add extra incentive for completion of this activity.)

"Tree Trimmings"

Preparation Directions:

1. Enlarge the rules below on tagboard.

2. Provide drawing paper, crayons, and one die.

3. Three players may play this game.

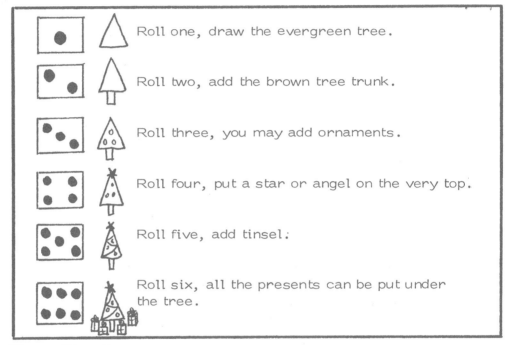

Roll one, draw the evergreen tree.

Roll two, add the brown tree trunk.

Roll three, you may add ornaments.

Roll four, put a star or angel on the very top.

Roll five, add tinsel.

Roll six, all the presents can be put under the tree.

Player Directions:

1. Each player takes a sheet of drawing paper, crayons, and pencil.

2. The die is rolled to see which player will go first.

3. The first player rolls the die. If he rolls one, he may begin his drawing. All the decorations must be added in numerical order.

4. The players take turns playing until one player finishes the decorating. That player wins the game!

JUST FOR FUN

On individual strips of tagboard, list
twenty-five presents the students
could receive for Christmas. Put
the strips in a stocking and instruct
the students to draw a present and
pantomime using that gift. See how
long it takes the class to guess this gift they
might receive.

Provide foil pie plates and scissors
and ask the students to cut out an
ornament to hang on the classroom
tree. They may wish to decorate
them with glitter. Provide string
for hanging the ornaments.

Mount a large construction paper tree
on a bulletin board. Decorate it with
colorful paper ornaments, doubled,
to be opened to reveal a printed message
in the center for each day in December.
The messages will reveal special treats
related to the holiday season. Some
messages might be popcorn, make
classroom decorations, select a
Christmas book for the teacher to read,
make Christmas cards for the principal
or some other special person, candy
canes for everyone, sing favorite
Christmas carols, etc. Select an
ornament each day and follow the
directions.

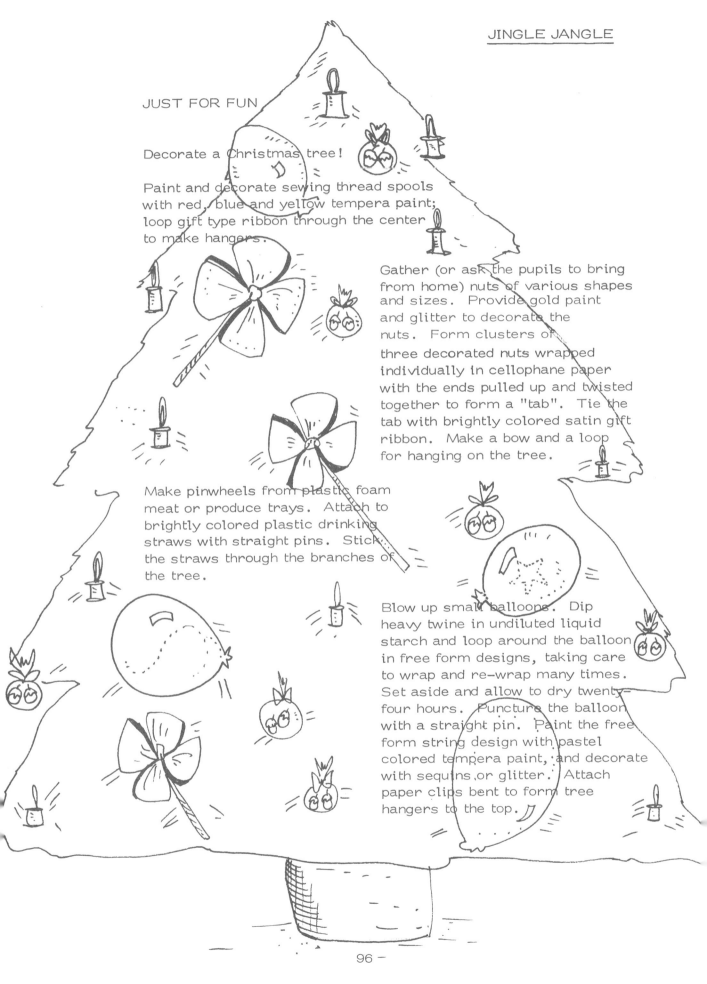

JUST FOR FUN

Decorate a Christmas tree!

Paint and decorate sewing thread spools with red, blue and yellow tempera paint; loop gift type ribbon through the center to make hangers.

Gather (or ask the pupils to bring from home) nuts of various shapes and sizes. Provide gold paint and glitter to decorate the nuts. Form clusters of three decorated nuts wrapped individually in cellophane paper with the ends pulled up and twisted together to form a "tab". Tie the tab with brightly colored satin gift ribbon. Make a bow and a loop for hanging on the tree.

Make pinwheels from plastic foam meat or produce trays. Attach to brightly colored plastic drinking straws with straight pins. Stick the straws through the branches of the tree.

Blow up small balloons. Dip heavy twine in undiluted liquid starch and loop around the balloon in free form designs, taking care to wrap and re-wrap many times. Set aside and allow to dry twenty-four hours. Puncture the balloon with a straight pin. Paint the free form string design with pastel colored tempera paint, and decorate with sequins or glitter. Attach paper clips bent to form tree hangers to the top.

JUST FOR FUN

Use a long table and appropriate art supplies to set up an art area for the following activities:

-   Design a vehicle for Santa in the year 2000.

-   Use screen wire, green paint, and spatter guns to spatter paint white construction paper trees. Glitter can be used for extra sparkle.

-   Use thread, glue, and construction paper to make Santa Claus mobiles.

-   Use popcorn, paste, red tempera paint and construction paper to make Santa portraits. (He could have a popcorn beard and moustache.)

-   Make Christmas stockings by cutting scraps of different kinds of materials into stocking shapes and gluing the sides together with rubber cement. Attach yarn loops for hanging. Fill with "goodies" before hanging on the tree.

Provide a cozy writing corner for students to retire to and use a story idea in their most creative fashion:

"How to have a litter-free Christmas"

"If you were an evergreen tree, what family would you like to be with on Christmas?"

"Santa's lost his sleigh..."

"Whew, you won't believe what happened in the workshop today!"

"I work in a candy cane factory."

Noteable New Years
Jan. 1
Jewish New Year
Year of the Tiger
Books
Costumes
Masquerade Ball
design a mask
NFL

IDNIGHT

ADNESS

12

"Resolution
Riters"

I pr?? e to
be?? ? better....

Display
Work Here

NFL

3X4

Happy New Year!

Ring out the old, ring in the new,
and may this be the best one yet.

CENTER PURPOSES:

After completing this center, the student should develop understanding and appreciation for New Year's Day through learning experiences in mask construction, writing resolutions, reports, and using multiplication and division facts.

CENTER ACTIVITIES:

Communications

"Resolution Riters"

Many years ago the people of England cleaned their chimneys on New Year's Day. This custom was supposed to bring good luck. Today we make resolutions resolving to make the New Year a better one than the old. Instruct the students to write resolutions incorporating but not restricted to the following ideas:

A resolution you want to make.

A resolution you should make.

A resolution you would like for your parents to make.

A resolution you would like for a friend to make.

A resolution you would like for your teacher to make.

A resolution you would like for your principal to make.

A resolution you would like for the President of the United States to make.

Creative Arts

"Masquerade Ball"

New Year's Eve is a time for parties and fun. At some parties people wear masks and do not reveal their identity until midnight. Provide the construction paper, crayons, paste, rubber bands and scissors to enable each student to make a creative mask. Guide the students in planning a New Year's Eve party. Divide the class into three groups. Ask one group to plan the games, one group to plan the refreshments, and one group to make decorations. To add a more festive mood, the students might enjoy wearing costumes to match their masks to the party.

Environmental Studies

"Notable New Years"

After the Gregorian Calendar was introduced, January 1 was designated as New Year's Day. The Jewish people and the Chinese people do, however, celebrate New Year's Day on different dates. Provide resource books to enable the students to read and compare January 1 as New Year's Day, the Jewish New Year, and the Chinese New Year. Instruct the students to use this information to write a report on the three New Years. Illustrating their reports will make them more interesting.

Quantitative Experience

"New Year's Bowl"

Football games are a New Year's Day tradition. Enjoy a different kind of football game in your classroom to celebrate this holiday. Draw a football field on a piece of tagboard. Make small footballs for markers. On index cards print multiplication and division facts. Print the following directions and place them in the center.

1. Each player takes a football marker and chooses a goal.
2. The markers are placed on the twenty-yard line.
3. The multiplication and division fact cards are shuffled and placed on the "sidelines".
4. One player draws a fact card and gives it to his opponent. If the opponent gives the correct answer he moves ten yards toward his goal. If he misses the fact, he moves ten yards back.
5. The games continues until one player scores a touchdown!

"Ring in the New Year"

Preparation Directions:

1. Enlarge the clock below on tagboard.

2. On index cards print words pertaining to New Year's Day.

3. Provide two markers and a small bell.

Player Directions:

1. Each player selects a marker and places it at 1:00.

2. The cards are shuffled and placed face down.

3. Taking turns, one player draws a card and gives the word to his opponent. If his opponent spells the word correctly, he moves one hour. If the player cannot spell the word, he does not move.

4. The first player to reach 12:00 wins. He can then ring the bell to welcome the New Year!

JUST FOR FUN

Provide art supplies to enable the students to make a crayon resist picture illustrating New Year's Eve.

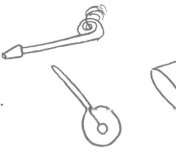

Provide song sheets and sing Auld Lang Syne. Appoint a committee to find out when this song was written, who wrote it, and any other interesting facts about the song.

Make a classroom portrait collage. Ask each student to draw himself in a setting to illustrate a resolution he has made. Display the collage attractively on a bulletin board.

walk the dog

wash the dishes

Instruct the students to work in groups of two to write poems about New Year's Day. Provide a time for sharing the poems.

Instruct the students to select a famous person (real or fictional) and make a New Year's resolution for him that might have changed the whole course of his life. Suggestions for starters might be:

Napoleon   Babe Ruth
George Washington Pope John
Alice in Wonderland Martin Luther King

Instruct the students to select one of the following ideas and write a creative story.

After eating blackeyed peas for good luck, I began...
At the New Year's Eve party, I suddenly...
As the bells were ringing, I heard a strange...
On New Year's Eve, I dreamed...

What's
the
Angle

square

arc circle

rectangle

write a
story using
these words
as puns.

Pun-ished
Players
school
shopping
sports
work

Fu
Pu

Exposure to
pun fun during a selected
week in January can provide
a good perk-up for the
post holiday return to school.

CENTER PURPOSES:

After completing this center, the student should develop awareness and appreciation of puns through learning experiences in art, writing creative puns, deciphering puns, and using mathematical terms.

CENTER ACTIVITIES:

Communications

"Pun-ished Players"

Make a list of topics from which the students may select one to write several puns about. Some topics might be:

school	shopping
sewing	play
plant life (nature)	sports
vacation	work
food	

Creative Arts

"Name Game"

Lead the group in a discussion of puns. Provide crayons, magic markers, scissors, paste and construction paper. Instruct the students to select one of the following "puns" on names to illustrate:

Bill Ding	Al-Phabet	Sue Per
Bobby Pins	Ray-Dio	Mary Land
Chuck Roast	Pam-Per	Carol Ling
Nick Nack	Sal A. Mander	Ted E. Bear

Environmental Studies

"Phonic Phumbles"

Ask the students to try to think of names of countries, cities, states and other places that lend themselves to a literal description. For example:

    Carlsbad, New Mexico: <u>Carls Bad</u> but not really terrible.
    Gobi Desert: <u>Gobi</u> whatever you want to be.
    Manila, Philippine Islands: Ice cream cones in strawberry,
                        chocolate and <u>manila</u>
    Calcutta, India: <u>Cal cutt a</u> picture out.

Provide art supplies for the students to use to illustrate their phonic phumbles.

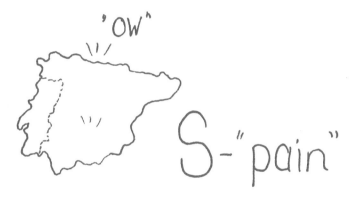

Quantitative Experience

"What's the Angle?"

Instruct the students to write a paragraph including puns with mathematical terms. Some terms they may wish to use are:

square	divide	numbers
arc	rectangle	add
circle	angle	area
parallel		triangle

"Fun Finders"

Can you find the puns and name the games or activity? Underline the puns.

1. Don't tee me off, this is a game for swingers.
    What's the game? _____

2. Everyone must pitch in to make this game a big hit.
    The game is _____

3. If you have some spare time, you might strike up an
    exciting afternoon when you _____

4. This might get you in over your head unless you master
    it. It's _____

5. With the right bounce, you'll net a big surprise.
    I am _____

6. This will keep you in stitches while bobbin' along.
    This is _____

7. I'm a hot subject, but usually get done.
    I'm _____

8. Don't rush into this unless you can tackle the subject.
    The sport is _____

9. If you get "board", you may be nailed for loafing.
    You could be a _____

10. It may be a dirty subject but the root of this may turn you
    green with envy. I'm a _____

JUST FOR FUN

To help the students better understand
puns, share with them the book Pun Fun
by Ennis Reas, Abelard-Schuman,
London, New York and Toronto, 1965.
Older students may enjoy reading James
Joyce and studying his style of writing.

Provide time for the students to
write animal riddles (often
puns may be written without
knowledge of the writer). Read
and analyze these riddles and
try to add puns.

Select a favorite story to be
rewritten by the class in a group
setting. Ask them to use as many
puns as possible in the rewriting.

Ask the students to keep a list
of all the puns they hear used
in the classroom during one
entire day. This day may be
called "pun-day", and the list
kept informally on the chalk
board.

1. Are you "board"?
2. "Chalk" it up to experience.
3. Math will "add" to your knowledge.
4. That "figures"! (at Math time)
5. Ecology is a "dirty" word.
6. Whew! Don't "pun"ish me!

Once the students begin to understand puns and their use, it may
be fun to make and illustrate a class anthology of puns.

Zodiac Signs
Cake Bake
Birthday Balloons
The mystery
I made a wis
On my birthday
I took a bite
Cake Bake
pick a ba
and write a
story
art
Monday's Horoscope
Libra

Party Time
Birthday Mail
U.S. MAIL
PICK UP TIMES
cake mix
HOW TO COOK
I made a wish and...
The Magic Birthday Cake...
Display Stories Here
Make a wish,
blow out the candles,
and sing a birthday song!

CENTER PURPOSES:

After completing this center, the student should develop awareness of the significance of birthdays through learning experiences in making birthday cards, writing creative stories, using signs of the zodiac and horoscopes, and making a cake.

CENTER ACTIVITIES:

Communications

"Birthday Balloons"

To add to a festive birthday mood, give each student a balloon to which a string and a small card has been attached. Print an idea designed to spark a creative story on each card. Some of the following ideas may be used:

The Mystery of the Missing Birthday Cake
The birthday party was a big success until...
I was surprised on my birthday when...
I made a wish and...
The Mysterious Birthday Gift
On my birthday the doorbell rang and...
The Magic Birthday Cake
On my birthday I feel...
I found a secret birthday message saying...
I took a bite of birthday cake and...

Creative Arts

"Just for You"

The birthday "student" can be made to feel very special by receiving greeting cards from his friends. Provide art supplies to be used in the creation of original birthday cards. Writing special birthday messages will make the cards personal. With brightly colored paper, cover a box to be used as a "mailbox" to be filled with cards and placed on the desk of the student who is having the birthday.

Environmental Studies

"Signs of the Time"

On a large piece of tagboard, draw the twelve signs of the zodiac. Lead a group discussion on the signs of the zodiac and horoscopes. Provide the necessary art materials to enable each student to draw his sign of the zodiac. Instruct the students to write horoscopes for the zodiac signs. Mount the signs of the zodiac on a bulletin board and encourage the students to share their horoscopes by displaying them on the same bulletin board.

Quantitative Experience

"Party Time"

No birthday is complete without a party! Provide two cake mixes, measuring cups, and cooking utensils. Divide the class into two groups and instruct each group to follow the directions to mix a cake and take it to the cafeteria to be baked. Let each group plan games, and when the cakes are done, enjoy a birthday party.

  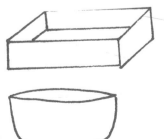

"Blow Out the Candles"

Preparation Directions:

1. Enlarge the cake below on tagboard.

2. Write each student's first name on an index card.

3. Provide two markers.

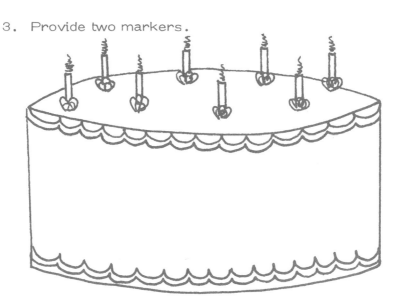

Player Directions:

1. Each player selects a marker.

2. Shuffle the cards and place them in a stack face down.

3. One player draws a card and reads the student's name on the card. He must give a noun, verb, and an adjective that begins with each letter of the name that is on the card. If the player can correctly do this, he moves to the first candle and "blows" it out.

4. Taking turns, continue to play until one person "blows" out all the candles.

JUST FOR FUN

Help the class to plan "special" gifts for the "birthday" student. An example of a "special" gift might be: sharing a book during library time, a listing of personal compliments, being first in line all day, having someone carry his books or hang up his coat.

Provide art supplies to enable the students to make symbolic birthday gifts to hang on a mobile for the birthday student to take home.

Help the students to write secret birthday messages to hide in the birthday student's desk.

Predict and draw what the student who is having a birthday will look like and what his job will be in fifteen years. Compile the pictures in a booklet to be presented to the birthday student as a special keepsake.

Provide resource books for the students to use to learn about the birth dates and birthplaces of famous people. A book for the classroom reading corner might be compiled and illustrated.

CENTER PURPOSES:

After completing this center, the
student should develop understanding
and appreciation for Groundhog Day
through learning experiences in
weather forecasting, map reading,
creative writing, and shadow play.

CENTER ACTIVITIES:

Communications

"Groundhog Gossip"

Ask the students to select one of the following ideas to use as
the theme for an imaginary story to be illustrated and placed
in a book for the school library:

"Have you heard what the Groundhog saw when he
peeked out his hole...?"

"Why was Gary Groundhog wearing sunglasses?"

"Oh no, it's February 10th! I've overslept."

"The best Groundhog Day Party I've ever been to was..."

Creative Arts

"Shadow Show"

Provide an overhead or a film strip projector to enable the
students to cast shadows on the wall. Instruct the students
to use their hands to make a silhouette of an animal for the
shadow show. The other students in the center will enjoy
trying to guess what animal shadow is being shown.

Environmental Studies

"Which Way?"

Provide a large map of the United States covered with
clear acetate.   Place it in the center and instruct the
students to locate Quarryville, Pennsylvania where the
Groundhog is supposed to appear each year. With a
grease pencil ask the students to mark the route from
their hometown to Quarryville, Pennsylvania. Using the
legend on the map, the students may compute the mileage
between these two points. Some students may want to
gather information enabling them to compare the cost of
travel by automobile, train, bus and plane, and plan an
imaginary trip to observe the Groundhog emerging.

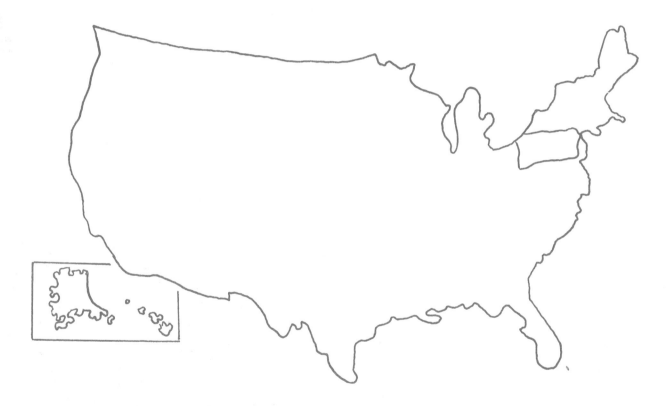

Quantitative Experience

"Cloudy or Clear"

Provide a thermometer, barometer, and a weather map
from the newspaper. Ask the students to record the weather
for Groundhog Day and use this information to forecast the
weather for February 3.

"Underground Playground"

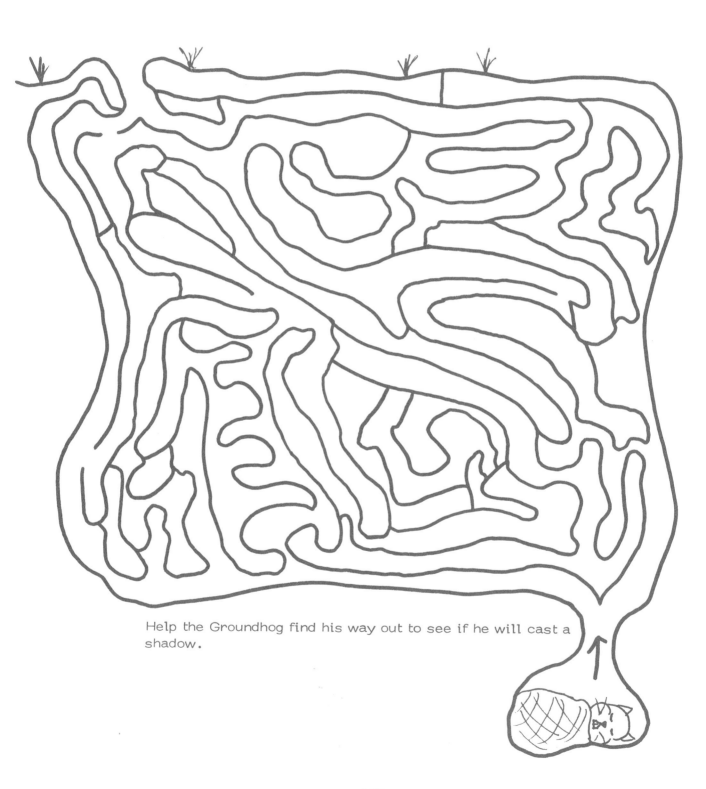

Help the Groundhog find his way out to see if he will cast a shadow.

JUST FOR FUN

Ask the students to draw a picture of a Groundhog in the clothes that depict the weather for the next six weeks.

Take the students outside to play Shadow Tag.

Provide time for the students to role play newspaper reporters interviewing a Groundhog.

Divide the students into small groups. Ask each group to read about the Groundhog and creatively portray his life style to the class. Pantomiming, a mural, a television quiz show, and an article for a nature magazine are suggestions that will motivate many other ideas.

Plan a contest to determine which student can compose the longest list of hibernating animals.

Some students might enjoy pretending to be Groundhogs and writing an autobiography. Take a class trip to a weather station to find out how the weather is scientifically predicted.

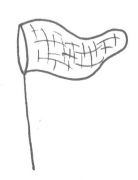

Display work here

Lin

Wide World of Lincoln

art

Mo

hou
ma
ye

While February 12 is not
recognized as a legal holiday
in many states, it is widely celebrated
as the birthday of a notable American.
On this day people of all ages continue to
pay tribute to the distinguished Civil
War president.

oln
Lore
irth date?
how old?
hizzes
?
Dear Abe,
Write a Letter
#1
make a peep show
Peep Shows
art

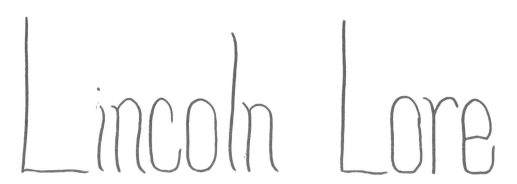

Lincoln Lore

CENTER PURPOSES:

> After completing this center, the student should have more knowledge and understanding of Abraham Lincoln through learning experiences in cardboard carpentry, letter writing, mental imagery and problem construction.

CENTER ACTIVITIES:

Communications

"Dear Abe"

To improve letter writing skills, instruct the students to write a letter to Abraham Lincoln. Instructions might include the following suggestions for ideas to be incorporated in the body of the letter:

where you live	your family
the type of clothes you wear	your home
the ways you spend your free time	your friends
your school--what you study	your chores
how you travel to school	your travels

Ask other students in the center to pretend they are Abraham Lincoln and answer the letters. Some of the following ideas might be included in these letters:

where Abraham Lincoln lived	his boyhood ambitions
the type of clothes he wore	his family
the ways he spent his free time	his home
his school--what he studied	his friends
how he traveled to school	his chores

Creative Arts

"Peep Show"

Provide shoe boxes and art supplies to enable the students to make a peep box. Divide the class into groups of three and ask each group to be responsible for planning and creating a peep box about one phase of Abraham Lincoln's life. Arrange time for the students to share and display the peep boxes. The peep boxes may then be arranged to show the events of Lincoln's life in the correct sequence of occurrence and displayed attractively to portray the life span of this great American.

Environmental Studies

"Wide World of Lincoln"

Place resource books in the center for the students to read about the life of Abraham Lincoln. Provide art supplies to enable the students to devise pictoral reports showing special events that happened during Lincoln's life and his presidency. The pictures can be put in a booklet and placed in a reading corner for everyone to enjoy.

Quantitative Experience

"Math Whizzes"

Place resource books in the center for the students to use to locate specific information. Instruct the students to write a math story problem or equation related to the following:

    The birth date and death date of Lincoln
    How many years Lincoln has been dead
    How old Lincoln was when he moved to Indiana
    How old Lincoln was when he moved to Illinois
    How old Lincoln was when he became a Congressman
    How old Lincoln was when he became President
    How many years did the Civil War last?
    The student's height compared with Lincoln's height

"Match the Logs"

Preparation Directions:

1. On strips of tagboard shaped like logs write the following
   questions and answers:

   Example:

   | Where was Lincoln born? | Hodgenville, Kentucky |

   | Lincoln's formal schooling was how long? | Less than one year |

   | After living in Kentucky, Lincoln and his family moved to what state? | Illinois |

   | A famous speech given by Lincoln | Gettysburg Address |

   | Lincoln's first job | Clerk in a store |

   | Lincoln's wife | Mary Todd |

   | What war was during Lincoln's presidency? | Civil War |

   | During which years was Lincoln president? | 1861–1865 |

   | A nickname given Lincoln | Honest "Abe" |

   | Where was Lincoln assassinated? | Ford's Theatre |

2. This activity is for one student.

3. Direct the student to shuffle the cards and try to match each
   question with the correct answer.

4. Provide an answer key for the student to use to check himself.

JUST FOR FUN

Provide art supplies for the students to use to draw two pictures of Lincoln. In one picture they should show Lincoln dressed in clothes of his day, and in the other picture show him dressed in mod clothes.

Ask the students to compare the duties of the president of the United States during Abraham Lincoln's presidency and now. After a group discussion on this topic, ask them to write an essay on "I'd rather be President _____ " (then or now) and state the reasons for their decision.

Provide resource books for the students to use to learn more about the Civil War. Ask them to role play Lincoln, a slave, a share cropper, a Confederate soldier, a Yankee general, a carpetbagger and other role descriptions associated with the period.

Play a game of "charades". Divide the class into small groups. Each group will decide a special event in Lincoln's life and pantomime it for the class.

Instruct the students to work in groups of three to plan and write a creative story using the title, "If I Were President". One student writes the first sentence, the second student writes the next sentence, and the third student writes the following sentence, etc. until the story is complete.

HEART♥

SWEET TREATS
...weigh the
candy......

Poetry
Pals

Pick a card
and make
a poem♡

PARTY

DISPLAY
WORK
HERE

love

happy

describe
your feelings
on hanging
valentines...

hanging
hearts

Valentine
Visions

make a
collage...

GLUE

mag-
azine

February 14 is Cupid's Day,
better known as Valentine's Day.
It is a time for hearts and
lace and secret
Valentine cards.

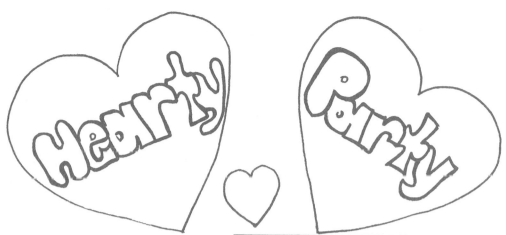

CENTER PURPOSES:

After completing this center, the student should develop appreciation for Valentine's Day through learning experiences in collages, creative writing, expressing emotions, and using a balance scale.

CENTER ACTIVITIES:

Communications

"Poetry Pals"

Cut heart shapes from tagboard and write one valentine word on each shape. Instruct the students to work with a classmate and write a poem by drawing a heart word card and including that word in a rhyming line. Have them continue drawing cards and writing lines until they have completed a valentine poem.

Creative Arts

"Valentine Visions"

Provide magazines and art supplies to enable the students to select pictures and words to make valentine collages. Remind the students to design collages conveying special valentine messages.

Environmental Studies

"Hanging Hearts"

Make a heart tree by collecting tree branches and painting them white. Secure the painted branches inside a large coffee can with plaster of paris. Cut red or pink heart shapes from tagboard and print one of the following words on each heart:

distrust   anxiety
love   envy
like   surprise
fear   friendliness
hate   groovy

happy

Hang the heart shapes on the tree with ribbons and instruct the students to select several hearts and tell how and why they may have this feeling on Valentine's Day. (They may want to "act out" the feelings or write original stories.)

Quantitative Experience

"Sweet Treats"

Place a small balance scale and fifteen candy hearts in the center. Instruct the students to find as many classroom objects as they can that will balance with the fifteen candy hearts. Have them estimate the weight of the hearts, then list five objects that are lighter and five objects that are heavier than the hearts. When this activity is completed, the students will enjoy eating the candy hearts. After all, Valentine's Day is a very special holiday.

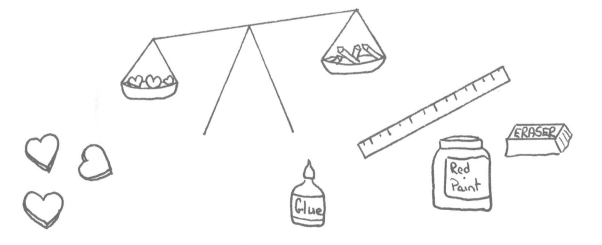

"King of Hearts"

Preparation Directions:

   1. Enlarge the game board below on tagboard.

   2. Prepare a deck of cards. On some cards paint one,
      two, or three red hearts. On several cards paint one
      green heart.

   3. Provide a marker for each player.

Player Directions:

   1. Place markers on the "starting" heart.

   2. Draw a card and move the number of hearts shown on
      the card. If you draw a green heart, go back two spaces.

   3. The first player around the board wins and becomes the
      "King of Hearts".

JUST FOR FUN

Younger students may enjoy making heart crowns to be worn
at the valentine party. Help them to cut hearts and glue them
on a white strip of construction paper. Staple the strip closed
and it's ready to be worn. (Older students might enjoy making
these valentine crowns to be presented to a kindergarten class
to be worn at their valentine party.)

Teachers can send very special
valentine cards to their students.
Print a special message on each
valentine, entitling the student
to a special privilege or job for
the day. The cards might be
honored any time between
February 1 and February 14.

Provide materials for the
students to use to create
collages from fabric, paper,
foil and other scrap box
material, with the stipulation
that all designs in the collage
must be heart-shaped.

Prepare a writer's corner and
let the students select a story
to write:

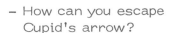

- How can you escape
  Cupid's arrow?

- What is the origin of the
  heart as a Valentine symbol?

- Why are valentines always
  pink and red?

- Help Cupid find his lost
  bow and arrow.

"Secret Senders"

Using the letters in V A L E N T I N E ' S   D A Y,
find out who is sending these valentinos.

JUST FOR FUN

Use an old deck of playing cards to make a "Queen of Hearts" game. Remove all queens except the Queen of Hearts. Four students may play this game using the "Old Maid" directions, drawing and matching until only the Queen of Hearts remains. The player holding this card wins the game.

Provide art supplies and scraps of lace, sequins, ribbons, glitter and beads for the students to use in designing fancy valentines. Print directions instructing the students to design valentines containing clues about themselves. Provide a box for secret valentines, then allow each student to draw one card at a time from the box to guess who the sender was. The valentines may be returned to the students to send to a special friend or relative.

Provide a flower box, pipe cleaners, and construction paper for the students to use to create a garden of hearts. Instruct them to fill the garden and then write a paragraph explaining how to care for and maintain the garden.

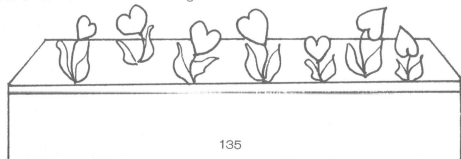

Write a story about George Washington's problems and display the stories

Decoders Delight

16 2 30   12 9 7   1 13 2 7 9

4 15 31 21 7   11 1 9 2

_ _ _ _ _   _ _ _   _ _ _ _ _

_ _ _   _ _ _   _ _ _ _ _

_ _ _ _   _ _ _ _

Pencil

Worries and Wonders

Wash
Write

Bake a cherry pie, stage a parade, prepare a patriotic address, or think of a more exciting way to celebrate the birthday of the first president of the United States.

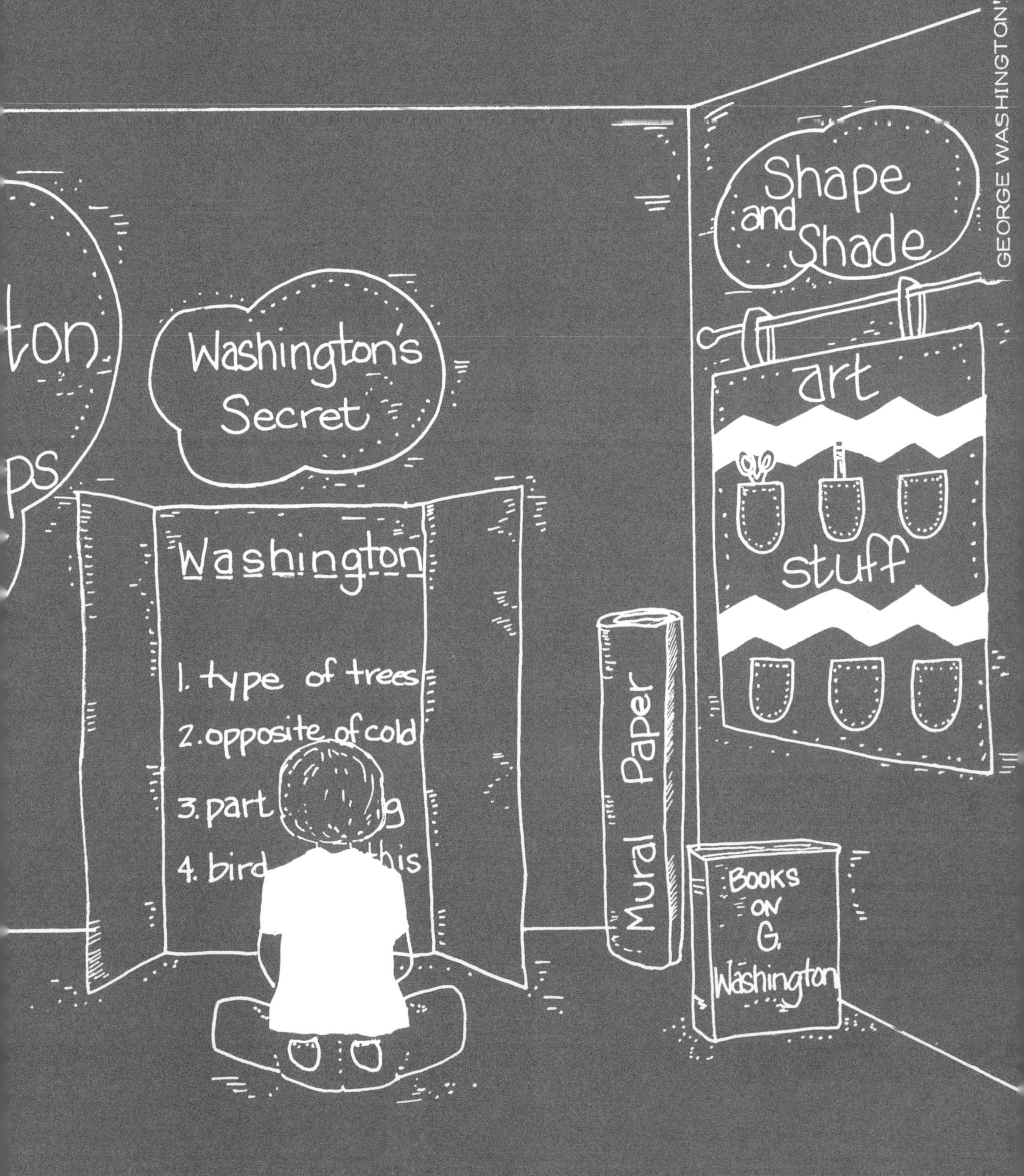
Washington's Secret
Washington
1. type of trees
2. opposite of cold
3. part
4. bird
Mural Paper
Books on G. Washington
Shape and Shade
art
stuff

CENTER PURPOSES:

> After completing this center, the student should develop appreciation for Washington's birthday through learning experiences in art, word games, and making inferences.

CENTER ACTIVITIES:

Communications

"Washington's Secret"

Instruct the students to use some of the letters in Washington to spell words that mean:

1. type of tree
2. opposite of cold
3. part of a leg
4. cans are made from this
5. birds do this
6. to hope for something
7. a carpenter's tool
8. to melt
9. children like to do this
10. a bee may do this
11. a kind of material
12. a large white bird
13. to act oneself
14. a small insect

Creative Arts

"Shape and Shade"

Provide mural paper or shelf paper and art supplies for students to trace and cut out their own shapes. Instruct them to use paint to "dress" the shape as George Washington might have dressed as a young boy, a surveyor, a general or President. Some girls may wish to do Martha Washington. Students may wish to work in small groups, and use resource books for more accurate pictures.

Environmental Studies

"Worries and Wonders"

Lead a group discussion related to George Washington as our country's first president. Ask the students to write about the problems he might have encountered as the first president. (They may list some of the advantages also.) Some of the students' work may be used as the basis for a panel discussion or a play.

Quantitative Experience

"Decoders Delight"

Instruct the students to solve this code that Washington might have sent his men while fighting in the Revolutionary War.

16 36 10   12   8   10   3   4   36   42 14   5   5
___ ___ ___ ___ ___ ___ ___ ___ ___   ___ ___ ___ ___

15   8   8   14 30   10   9   6   6   3   16   6
___ ___ ___ ___ ___ ___   ___ ___ ___ ___   ___ ___

36 10   5   7   20   9   12   14 18 36 16
___ ___ ___ ___ ___ ___   ___ ___ ___ ___ ___

16 36 10   2   8   14 16 14   9   36   42 10
___ ___ ___   ___ ___ ___ ___ ___ ___ ___   ___ ___

42 14   5   5   42 14   4   16 36 10
___ ___ ___ ___ ___ ___ ___   ___ ___ ___

42 15   8 .
___ ___ ___

A – 3 x 5	H – 6 x 6	R – 56 – 7
B – 2 x 1	I – 7 x 2	S – 3 x 3
C – 24 – 6	L – 40 – 8	T – 4 x 4
E – 2 x 5	N – 24 – 8	U – 4 x 5
F – 4 x 3	O – 12 – 2	V – 5 x 6
G – 3 x 6	P – 28 – 4	W – 7 x 6

"Mount Vernon Mystery"

Across:

3. He was our first _____.
5. Known as _____ of our country.
8. His rank in the army was _____.
10. Was born in 173___.
11. Presidental term was _____ years.
13. Married _____ Custis.
15. When a young boy, worked as a _____.

Down:

1. City named after him.
2. Helped to form the United _____.
4. Fought in the _____ War.
5. Spent a cruel winter with his troops in Valley _____.
6. His home was Mount _____.
7. Birthday in the month of _____.
9. His home was on the _____ River.
12. Chopped down a _____ tree when a boy.
14. Served as general in the _____.

JUST FOR FUN

Bake cherry pies at school lunch time. Make it easy prepared shells and cherry to be enjoyed at by using already pie filling.

Ask the students to contrast the way of life during Washington's time and now. Change your classroom routine to allow the students to experience education as it was in the 1750s.

Instruct the students to write to Mt. Vernon, Virginia to obtain literature about Washington's home.

If possible plan a field trip to a museum of history to discover the way of living in the 18th century. Compare life in your part of the country at that time to life in Mt. Vernon. If a trip to the museum is not possible, use resource books to secure information to carry out the activity.

Using mural paper and art supplies, let students depict the important events in George Washington's life.

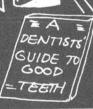

Creamy Toothpaste

The Brush Off

CENTER PURPOSES:

After completing this center, the
student should know the rules of good
dental health through learning
experiences in using resource books,
nouns and adjectives, making graphs,
and presenting a puppet show.

CENTER ACTIVITIES:

Communications

"Dental Describers"

Divide the students into two groups. Instruct one group to
make a list of nouns that are related to dental health. Instruct
the second group to make a list of adjectives. After a period
of ten minutes, instruct the groups to exchange lists.

To the noun list, adjectives must be added, and to the
adjective list nouns must be added to make good dental
health words.

Example:	Nouns	Adjectives	Words
	teeth	white	white teeth
	apples	red	red apples

Creative Arts

"The Big Bag"

Provide art supplies and paper bags to enable the students to
make puppets. Instruct the students to create a character that
could be used to show good dental health. Some ideas for
characters are: boy, tooth, healthy foods, dental hygienist;
girl, dentist, toothbrush. After the puppets are completed,
ask the students to prepare a script for a puppet show. Arrange
a time for sharing the puppet shows.

Environmental Studies

"The Answer, Please"

Place resource books in the center and allow time for the
students to read about teeth and good dental health. Instruct
each student to write one question concerning good dental
health on a strip of paper. On the back of the question the
student should write the answer. Provide a covered box in
which the students may place the questions and answers. At
a given time the students may stage a make-believe TV
quiz program using their questions and answers.

Quantitative Experience

"Fun Flossers"

Prepare the following check list for the students to use to take
a dental health poll:

> brush teeth at least twice a day
> use dental floss
> visit dentist twice a year
> drink milk three times a day
> have at least eight permanent teeth
> do not have a cavity

Instruct the students to use the results of the poll to make a graph.

"Tooth Teasers"

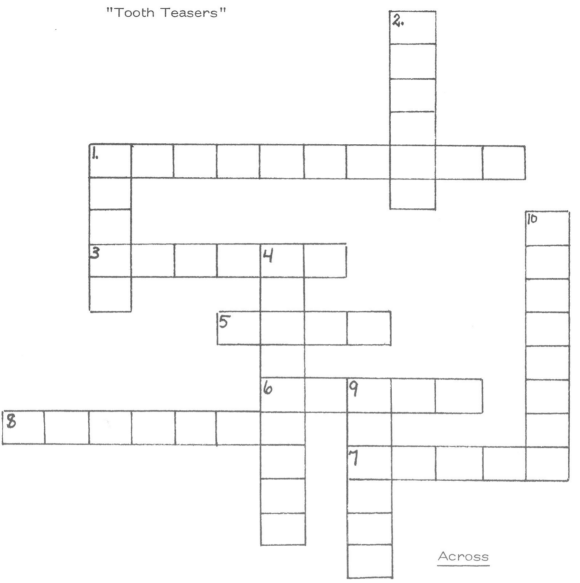

Down

1. You should visit your dentist _____ a year

2. Part of the tooth between enamel and root

4. The number of permanent teeth

9. The hard covering of the tooth

10. Adding this to water helps prevent tooth decay

Across

1. We hide our teeth under the pillow for the _____

3. Sweets cause this

5. Best food for building strong teeth

6. Everyone has two sets

7. If you don't have a toothbru eating an _____ is good

8. The first set of teeth is called _____ teeth

JUST FOR FUN

Invite a dentist to speak to the class during "Dental Health Week".

Provide art supplies to enable the students to draw one food that builds strong teeth. Use the pictures to make a class collage.

The students might enjoy writing a television commercial about dental health. Provide time for illustrating and sharing the commercials.

Instruct the students to write a creative story using one of the following ideas:

"The Conversation Between My Teeth"

"What the Toothbrush Said to the Teeth"

"How the Teeth Felt After Chewing Gum"

Using the tune "Here We Go 'Round the Mulberry Bush", instruct the students to create original songs to encourage good dental health.

Parade

Guess the Guise

Tribal Tributes

Disguises

BOOKS

of
oes

Select
a
Superstar

Satchmo

Hank
Aaron

Nat
King
Cole

Aretha
Franklin

musical

moods

Celebrating Black History
Week during the month of February
gives Americans an opportunity to
recognize and pay respect to
black men and women
important to our country's heritage.

CENTER PURPOSES:

After completing this center, the student should develop appreciation for Black History Week through learning experiences in writing biographical reports, appreciative listening, comparing life styles and computing averages.

CENTER ACTIVITIES:

Communications

"Guessing the Guise"

Provide a list of famous black people, past or present. Athletes, musicians, scientists, or politicians may be included in this list. Have the students use resource books to prepare reports on one of the famous people. The students may wish to dress up as their "hero" to read their report and have their classmates try to guess who they are.

Creative Arts

"Musical Moods"

Set up a listening station with records, record player, and headphones. Provide records that are sung by black artists known for singing "soul" or the "blues" songs. Instruct the students to listen to a record and write a short paragraph about their mood while listening to the record.

Environmental Studies

"Tribal Tribute"

Select an African tribe and provide resource books about the tribe. Instruct the students to study their environment, traditions, customs, daily habits, religion, and government. Ask them to use the information gathered in contrasting their way of life to the life of a tribal boy or girl, and to write a story, play or poem emphasizing the likenesses as well as the differences in the two life styles.

Quantitative Experience

"Super Stars"

Provide the students with the following problems and instruct them to compute the average for each problem.

1. O. J. Simpson gained 2000 yards last year playing in fourteen football games. How many yards did he average per game?

2. At the close of the 1973 baseball season Hank Aaron had batted in 713 home runs. He has played for twenty years, averaging how many home runs per year?

3. In three basketball games, Walt Frazier shot 29 points, 35 points, and 22 points. How many points did he average per game?

4. What is the average height in inches of these three famous basketball players:

Wilt Chamberlain	7'1"
Bill Russell	6'10"
Earl Monroe	6'3"

"Pyramid of Heroes"

Complete this pyramid by filling in the answers to the clues of famous black heroes.

1. Well-known boxer who changed his name.
2. Great civil rights leader.
3. Broke Babe Ruth's home run record.
4. Great scientist.
5. Great football running back.
6. First black to play baseball.
7. Always sang the blues and played a trumpet.
8. Pushed for education for the Blacks, leader at Tuskegee.
9. Also called Wilt the Stilt.
10. Well-known woman tennis and golf player.

JUST FOR FUN

Provide art supplies for the students to use to draw portraits of black heroes. Mount the portraits on a bulletin board with the heading "Parade of Heroes".

Read from the book I Am the Darker Brother, an anthology of modern poems by American Negroes, MacMillan Co., 1968.

Make a list of books, songs and poems written by Negro writers. Print this list on a chart and mount it in the library corner.

Prepare an assembly program consisting of songs and poems written by Negro authors, and present it to another class.

Bring records to the classroom and plan a "sing-along" featuring music by Negro musicians.

Ask the students to use resource books from the library to gather information about contributions made to our present-day way of life by black Americans in times past. Remind them to be on the lookout for inventors, statesmen, soldiers, etc.

Ask the students to make an illustrated list of famous black women.

Kiss and Tell
I found....
Walking...
I forgot...
The best...
EMERALD ISLE ......
WRITE A DIARY.....
LEPRE
art

DISPLAY PICTURES HERE
GRAPH
IRE LAND
Rejoice and make merry!
'Tis no blarney that the Luck of the Irish abounds on Saint Patrick's Day.

Leaping Leprechaun

CENTER PURPOSES:

> After completing this center, the student should develop appreciation for Saint Patrick's Day through learning experiences in planning imaginary travels, graphing, creative writing and art.

CENTER ACTIVITIES:

Communications

"Kiss and Tell"

Print the following ideas on a chart and ask the students to select one to use as the theme for a creative story:

I found a four-leaf clover and...
I kissed the blarney stone and...
The best way to catch a leprechaun is...
Waking up on Saint Patrick's Day, everything suddenly
   turned green...
I forgot to wear green on Saint Patrick's Day...

Creative Arts

"Hide and Seek"

Tell a leprechaun story! Provide mural paper, orange, brown, and green tempera paint, and brushes for the students to use to illustrate leprechauns and their favorite hiding places. Arrange an attractive bulletin board for displaying the mural.

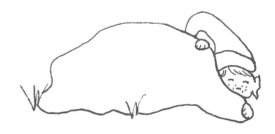

Environmental Studies

"Emerald Isle"

Instruct the students to take an imaginary trip to Ireland, and keep a daily diary of the places they see and their exciting adventures while there. Place maps and reference books in the center to provide the factual information needed.

Quantitative Experiences

"Greenery Graph"

Instruct the students to make a bar graph showing:

1. the number of students wearing green.

2. the number of green pencils being used in the classroom.

3. the number of students whose favorite color is green.

4. the number of students whose parents have a green car.

5. the number of students who use a green toothbrush.

6. the number of students who have a green room at home.

7. the number of students whose favorite lollipop is lime.

Provide watercolors for the students to mix an original shade of green to use to complete their graph.

"Pot of Gold"

Preparation Directions:

1. Enlarge the game board on tagboard.
2. On index cards, write the following words:

Irish	Blarney Stone	Leprechaun
green	shamrock	four-leaf clover
lucky	charm	Ireland
march	gold	Saint Patrick's Day
(other words may be added)		

3. Provide two markers.

Player Directions:

1. Each player selects a marker and places it on the game board.
2. The cards are shuffled and placed face down. Taking turns, one player draws a card, reads the word, and asks his partner to spell it. If the player spells the word correctly, he moves one space.
3. The first player to reach the "pot of gold" wins the game.

JUST FOR FUN

Arrange for the students to prepare a
Saint Patrick's Day dinner menu using
only green food.

Prepare some shamrock cookies and
lime punch for a special surprise.

A simple recipe for sugar cookies is:

2-1/2 c. flour
1 tsp. baking powder
1/2 tsp. salt
1 c. shortening
1 c. sugar
2 eggs
1-1/2 tsp. vanilla

Cream sugar and shortening.
Add eggs one at a time, and
vanilla. Sift dry ingredients
and add. Mix well, chill,
roll out and cut out in shamrock
shapes. Bake at 350 degrees
10-12 minutes. Makes 7-1/2
dozen. Frost with green
confectioner sugar icing.

Students may write their own
Saint Patrick's Day play and
invite their parents to the performance.
Invite an Irishman to come to the classroom to share some "blarney" about Ireland
with the students.

Provide construction paper, scissors, paste, buttons, and junk
materials for the students to use to create unique good luck charms.

Using styrofoam cups, green
pipe cleaners, green construction
paper, and styrofoam cubes ask
each student to make a pot of
shamrocks for his desk. The
shamrocks can be cut from green
paper and glued to a pipe cleaner
to form a stem. The styrofoam
cube in the bottom of each cup
will serve as a flower holder.

Read some poetry by well known Irish poets to inspire young poets
to create some of their own poems about Saint Patrick's Day.
Mount their poems on large green shamrocks.

Spring Whing-Ding

put story in proper sequence

Spring Signs

make a mobile

baseball

bird

Kite

garden

bare-foot

Spring Sequence

Living things, green and growing, herald the arrival of Spring. Winter's gone and the promise of blue skies and sunny days is in the air.

Spring Whing-Ding

CENTER PURPOSES:

> After completing this center, the student should develop sensitive awareness of Spring through learning experiences in sequencing, revolution of the earth, money and making mobiles.

CENTER ACTIVITIES:

Communications

"Spring Sequence"

Select a story about Spring. Cut the sentences apart, paste them on strips of tagboard, and place them in an attractively covered box. Instruct the students to arrange the sentences in correct sequence to make the story complete. Supply an answer key for the students to use to check themselves. Provide strips of tagboard and instruct the students to write a paragraph about Spring, writing one sentence on each tagboard strip. Place the paragraph in an envelope and ask another student to arrange the paragraph in correct sequence and illustrate it.

Creative Arts

"Spring Signs"

On the first day of Spring lead a class discussion focusing on signs of Spring. Make a list of the signs suggested by the group. Some of the following ideas might be included:

kites	Easter	baseball
new clothes	making a garden	birds
flowers	Spring vacation	blooming trees
	going barefoot	

Instruct the students to use one of the signs of Spring as the idea for one section of a mobile. Provide tagboard, tissue paper, paste, paint, cord and coat hangers for construction of the mobiles. Assemble and hang them from the ceiling for everyone to enjoy.

Environmental Studies

"Spinning Seasons"

Lead a group discussion explaining how seasonal changes
are caused by the movement of the earth around the sun.
Provide balloons, strips of newsprint, paste and tempera
paints. Divide the class into five groups and ask four groups
to make a model of the earth and one group to make a model
of the sun. Using the completed models, allow time for the
students to demonstrate the changes of seasons. Arrange the
models on a table and encourage the students to explore the
earth's revolution around the sun by manipulating the models.

Quantitative Experience

"Spring Spenders"

Everyone enjoys buying a new Spring outfit. Provide a
catalog and written instructions telling the students that
they have $60.00 to spend on Spring clothes. Ask them
to itemize each piece of clothing, the cost, and then tabulate
the amount spent. Remind them that the total must not
exceed $60.00.

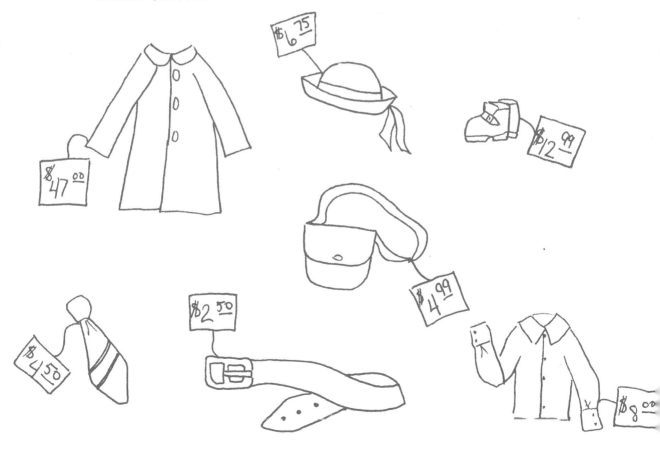

"Spring Blends"

Using tagboard, cut three circles to be used as the centers of flowers.
On each circle write the consonant blend "spr".

Make sixteen tagboard petals. On each
petal print the following endings:

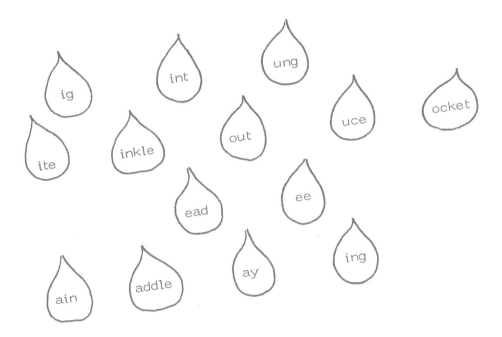

Place the circles and petals in an envelope. Instruct the students
to make a flower by matching the consonant blend "spr" with an
ending to form a word. Ask the students to write a sentence with
each word.

JUST FOR FUN

Ask the students to use some
of the following ideas to write
a creative story:

What the puff of wind said to
the kite.

How the worm felt when the
garden was planted.

Conversation between new
spring clothes in a store.

What an empty classroom says
during Spring vacation.

Enjoy making a "spring" crayon
resist picture. Draw the picture
with crayons. Then use light blue
tempera paint to paint over the
picture.

Have a Spring Fashion Show. The students do not have
to be wearing new clothes, but must describe their outfits
and the material from which it is made. Provide background music for the show.

Plant a "Story Garden".
Encourage the students to
write a story about something
that happens in the Spring.
Provide art supplies for the
students to design and make
a book jacket for their story.
Paste the story inside the
book jacket. Prepare a
bulletin board to represent a
garden and arrange the stories
attractively on it.

wildlife

animal critters

SIMILIE
SOUND
OFF

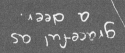

graceful as
a deer

Celebrated during
one week in March, National
Wildlife Week is the perfect time
to reflect on the influence of our
changing environment on wildlife.

CENTER PURPOSES:

> After completing this center, the student should develop appreciation for National Wildlife Week through learning experiences in art, writing similes, studying extinct animals, and graphing.

CENTER ACTIVITIES:

Communications

"Simile Sound-off"

Place a study guide about similes in the center and ask the students to write similes about animals.

Example: graceful as a deer
fluffy white as a swan

The similes may be printed on 9 x 12 sheets of white construction paper and illustrated with crayon drawings to be bound in a book entitled "Animal Similes". A brown cardboard cover, green lettering, and a leather boot string for lacing will help to connect the completed pages into an attractive addition to the classroom free reading shelf.

Creative Arts

"Animal Menagerie"

Collect pictures of animals from old magazines. Cut the heads off all the animals and make the pictures available to the students. Instruct the students to select a picture, glue it on construction paper, and use crayons or chalk to draw the head on the animal. After the heads have been drawn, the animal should be identified by name and labeled accordingly. The students might also profit from using the back of the sheet to draw the animal in its natural habitat.

Environmental Studies

"Animal Exit"

Provide resource books and a list of extinct animals or animals whose survival is threatened. Challenge the students to discover the causes of extinction for these particular animals. Ask them to try to provide solutions to save these animals from extinction, and to design posters promoting these solutions.

Quantitative Experience

"Trips 'n Travels"

Instruct the students to use resource books to discover the distance that some animals and birds migrate. Let them select five animals to research and to record the data in graph form to show which animal migrates the farthest.

"Sanctuary Safety"

Preparation Directions:

1. Enlarge the game board below on tagboard.

2. Prepare a deck of game cards. On each card print the name of an insect, bird, fish, amphibian, reptile, or mammal.

3. Provide a marker for each player.

4. Three or four students may play this game.

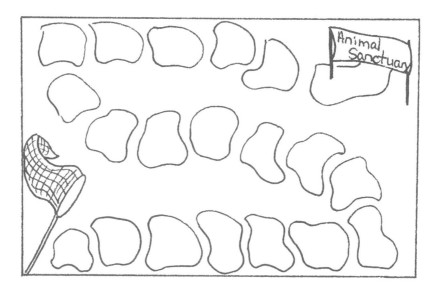

Player Directions:

1. The cards are shuffled and placed face down on the game board.

2. The first player draws a card. If he can identify the kind of animal it is, he may move one space.

        Example: oriole = bird

If he misses the identification, he must remain where he is.

3. The first player to reach the animal sanctuary wins the game!

JUST FOR FUN

Take the students on a field trip to a nearby zoo, aquarium, wildlife preserve, or woodland. Prepare an information sheet for the students to take with them to help in the observation of particular animal habits and characteristics.

Provide thirty minutes for the students to observe wildlife in the school yard. Have a contest to see which student can make the most extensive wildlife list.

Instruct the students to cut pictures of animals from magazines. The pictures may be glued on construction paper, and crayons, chalk or tempera paint used to fill in the correct background to show the animals' natural environment.

Mount a large world map on a bulletin board. On small strips of tagboard, write names of animals that are unfamiliar to the students. Have a contest to see who can pin the unusual animals to their homeland. Provide research books.

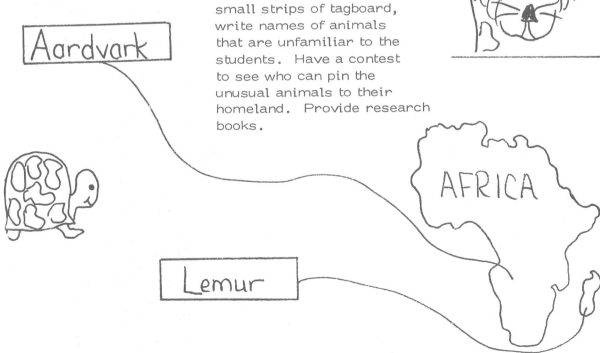

Timely Jokes
- write and illustrate an April Fool joke...
1500
1600
1700
1800
1900
2000
Fool Follies
Fool Fu
design a costume
Once upon a time

Fantastic Foolers
General Store
April Auction
bid one spelling word
April Fool story
No foolin', April Fool's Day is celebrated the world over by pranksters and practical jokers. It is a good time to relax and have a little fun.

CENTER PURPOSES:

After completing this center, the student should develop awareness of April Fool's Day through experiences in writing and producing original plays, using time lines, and in consumer marketing.

CENTER ACTIVITIES:

Communications

"April Auction"

April Fool's Day is a time for fun and games. The students will enjoy staging an auction, complete with items they have made. Provide boxes of all sizes, styrofoam, toothpicks, scraps of material, blocks of wood, tagboard, nails, paints, glue, and other art materials to enable each student to create a three-dimensional object. This object could be a toy, a food, a game, an animal, or any other whimsical thing. Display the objects attractively. With the teacher acting as the auctioneer, the students can bid on the three-dimensional objects. Instead of using money they must bid spelling words. If an object brings four spelling words, the teacher will give the student four words to spell. If the student correctly spells the words, he may keep the object. If the words are not spelled correctly, the next highest bidder has a chance to spell the words. The auction continues until all items have been sold.

Creative Arts

"Fool Follies"

Divide the class into five groups and instruct each group to write a short play with the plot focusing on an April Fool's joke. Provide cardboard, paste, paints, scissors, crepe paper and "junk" for students to use to make scenery and simple costumes. Set aside a special time for each group to present their play.

Environmental Studies

"Timely Jokes"

Provide resource books to enable the students to read and understand the origin of April Fool's Day. Prepare a time line from 1500 – 2000 and place it on a bulletin board. Instruct the students to write and illustrate an April Fool joke that might have occurred during a period on the time line. Mount the illustrated jokes attractively on the time line.

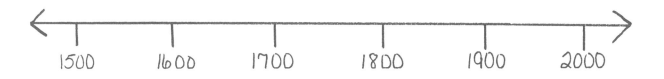

1500   1600   1700   1800   1900   2000

Quantitative Experience

"Fantastic Foolers"

In a quiet corner of the room prepare a table or shelves to be used as a store. Instruct the students to bring a wrapped object from home to sell in the store. Explain that the object is to be funny so it will be a joke when opened. Divide the class into four groups. Ask one group to be responsible for designing and making the store sign; another group to be responsible for arranging the wrapped objects on the shelves; one group to be responsible for pricing the objects for sale; and the last group to be responsible for making play money to be used in purchasing the objects. Give each student $2.00 in play money, and provide time for all students to shop for an April Fool gift. Sharing the gifts as they are unwrapped will provide laughs and group interaction.

"Jokeville"

Preparation Directions:

1. Enlarge the game board below on tagboard, and provide three markers.
2. Write the following sentences on strips of tagboard.

There's a purple rabbit.
Move one space.

No school on April Fool's Day.
Take an extra turn.

It's raining ice cream cones.
Move two spaces.

The car has no driver!
Lose one turn.

The cat is barking.
Move one space.

The hamburger spoke to me.
Move one space.

The book had invisible words.
Move two spaces.

You've just won a trip
around the world.
Take another turn.

The soda pop was magic.
Move back one space.

You've won a new car.
Move one space.

You're buying everyone a candy bar.
Move two spaces.

You get to go to bed as late
as you wish.
Move one space.

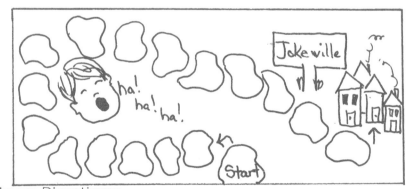

Player Directions:

1. Each player selects a marker and places it on "Start".
2. The cards are shuffled and placed face down in a stack.
3. Taking turns, players draw a card and move the number
   of spaces indicated.
4. The first player to reach "Jokeville" wins the game.

JUST FOR FUN

Students might enjoy making an April Fool's Day menu. The foods used should be imaginative, but edible. One recipe could be included in the menu.

Ask the students to use one of the following ideas to write a creative April Fool's story.

I was taking my pet tiger for a walk and...

It was April Fool's Day and the teacher...

I couldn't believe what I saw as I...

Instruct the students to make up riddles about each other. The riddles may be nonsensical or untrue, but must provide enough real clues to make the student identifiable.

Provide resource books and ask the students to research the origin of April Fool's Day. They might then enjoy writing original stories, songs or poems about the people and events of the first April Fool's Day.

Provide paper and charcoal, or black construction paper and white chalk for the students to use to draw facial expressions showing a victim of an April Fool's joke. Illustrate facial expressions showing surprise, happiness, hostility, fright, frustration, and disbelief. Display the pictures attractively.

SAVE THE AIR

READ

REBIRTH

PAINT A ROCK

Rocks Renewed

Earth Week is celebrated in April. This is a good time to express appreciation for the environment and its resources.

CENTER PURPOSES:

> After completing this center, the student should develop appreciation for Earth Week through learning experiences in art, letter writing, pollution solutions, and recycling.

CENTER ACTIVITIES:

Communications

"Information Station"

Instruct the students to write letters to local environmental groups asking for information, posters and pamphlets. The acquired materials may be used to develop an environmental information booth in the classroom.

Creative Arts

"Rocks Renewed"

Arrange a working area and provide the following supplies:

flat, smooth rocks	acrylic paints
brushes	turpentine
shellac	

Instruct the students to paint their favorite living thing (person, animal or plant) on the top of a rock. After letting it dry, they may shellac the rock to keep the picture from chipping. The "renewed rocks" may be used for paperweights.

Environmental Studies

"City Solutions"

Hang mural paper on a large bulletin board and provide art supplies for the students to use to paint a city scene.

Instruct the students to study the city scene and write a paragraph listing objects they see that are polluting our environment. Ask them to devise solutions to the problems they see and list them on a chart to be displayed beside the mural.

Quantitative Experience

"Recycled Recipes"

Lead a group discussion related to recycling and let the students give examples of recycled materials.

Instruct the students to select one item they feel needs to be recycled and illustrate the recycling process they would use. Ask them to include every necessary step, and then write the steps on a recipe card.

"Pollution Pests"

Preparation Directions:

1. Enlarge the game board below on tagboard, making a symbol in every space. The fish represents water, the flower represents the earth, and the balloon represents air.

2. Prepare a deck of cards and on every card write a pollution problem that harms the air, the water or the earth.

     Example: dirty smoke stack   strip mining   detergent

3. Provide a marker for each player.

Player Directions:

1. Place the markers on the starting arrow.

2. Shuffle the playing cards and place them face down on the board.

3. The first player draws a card, reads the pollution problem, and must tell if it harms the water, air, or land. If he answers correctly, he moves to the proper symbol. If he misses, he moves back one space.

4. The players take turns until one player reaches "Clean City" and wins the game.

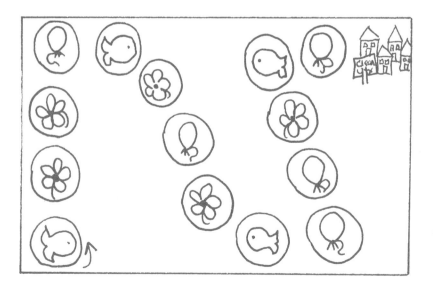

JUST FOR FUN

Take students on a field trip to a nursery or florist. Each student may wish to buy a small plant or together buy a class plant. Use resource books to find out how to take care of the plants.

Help the students to plan and carry out a clean-up project. They may be a neighborhood area that needs to be cleaned up, or they may wish to clean up the school. Talk to the city council about sponsoring a recycling center for newspapers, glass, or aluminum.

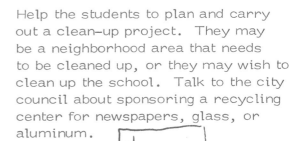

Invite a resource person from a local environmental group or agency to speak to the class. Students may wish to discuss and prepare some questions for the speaker.

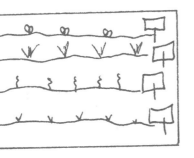

Ask the principal for a small plot of land in the schoolyard that could be converted into a garden. Assist the students in plotting out their garden, what they will grow, when they can plant, and how they will care for the garden. On a smaller scale, plant garden vegetables in the classroom. Plastic bleach containers make good planters.

Have a contest to see which students can identify the types of trees in the schoolyard. Take a walking field trip to observe all the types of trees in the neighborhood. See if they can match the proper nut or fruit to each tree.

Provide art supplies for the students to use to make posters about Earth Week. Talk to city merchants about letting students hang posters in their windows to inform people about Earth Week. Ask students to pick and press flowers and leaves in heavy books. After the flowers have dried, provide construction paper, waxed paper, iron, and scissors to enable the students to make their own stationery. Instruct the students to fold the construction paper in half and on the top page arrange the dried flowers and leaves. Place a sheet of waxed paper over this and apply heat from the iron until the waxed paper is fastened to the card.

Display work

"bunny bonanza"

How to make breakfast

eggs

pick an egg and write a story

you have

what Christmas

You have

Write an

Baskets full of eggs,
Easter bonnets galore,
fuzzy chicks and cuddly rabbits
herald the Easter parade.

EASTER
AROUND
THE
WORLD

Easter
in
France

Easter
in
GERMANY

how many? how
Egg many.

Estimaters

Guess the
number of
beans.

CENTER PURPOSES:

> After completing this center, the student should develop appreciation for Easter through learning experiences in cooking, making mosaics, writing creative stories, presenting oral reports, and estimating.

CENTER ACTIVITIES:

Communications

"Sunny Side Up"

Make a large paper mache or newspaper strip Easter egg to hold the story ideas.

Instruct the students to open the Easter egg and select one of the following ideas to use as the theme for a creative story, poem, song or play:

What Christmas job could the Easter Bunny hold?

Write an autobiography about your life as a jelly bean.

You have just landed on Pluto and it's Easter! Plan an Easter celebration for the planet.

You have been shipwrecked on an island where there are no Easter goodies. Tomorrow is Easter and you must fill a basket for a friend. Describe what you will use.

Creative Arts

"Scrambled Eggs"

Enjoy a second breakfast at school! Provide eggs, a mixing bowl, spoon, electric skillet, paper plates and plastic forks. Divide the class into four task groups to prepare and scramble

the eggs. One group may crack the eggs; one group may
beat the eggs; one group may cook the eggs; one group
may serve the eggs...and everyone may eat the eggs!
Toast or sweet rolls may be served with the eggs. After
the eggs have been eaten instruct the students to wash and
dry the egg shells. Prepare food coloring or Easter egg
dye for coloring the egg shells. Instruct the students to
crush the egg shells and provide construction paper and glue
for making an Easter mosaic. Display the mosaics
attractively.

Environmental Studies

"Easter Parade"

Lead a group discussion on "Easter Around the World".
Provide resource books and instruct students to select a
country and prepare an oral report on Easter customs of
that country. Provide time for students to present their
reports to the group. They may wish to wear a costume
from the selected country, and make posters, charts or
other autio-visual aids to make the reports more interesting.

Quantitative Experience

"Egg Estimaters"

Lead a group discussion to compare and contrast the meaning
and use of an estimate and an exact number. Fill one jar
with jelly beans and place in the center. Provide a pound
scales. Print the following directions on tagboard and mount
them on the bulletin board. Instruct the students to follow directions.

1. Look carefully at one jar of jelly beans.
   Estimate the number of jelly beans.
2. Count the jelly beans to find an exact number.
   Write an equation and compute your answer to show
   the difference between your estimated answer and
   your exact answer.
3. Estimate the weight of one jar of jelly beans.
4. Using the scales, find the exact weight of the jar of
   jelly beans. Write an equation and compute your answer
   to show the difference between your estimated answer
   and your exact answer.

"Treasure Hunt"

Print the following messages to place inside plastic Easter eggs.

4. Check the window... that's a good place for a clue to be hidden!

1. Look behind the third book on the bookshelf.

2. Get a drink of water; then follow a straight line to the chalkboard.

5. Go to the creative writing center for the next directions.

3. It might be a good idea to sharpen your pencil.

6. Sorry, keep looking. Have you checked under the teacher's desk?

7. Write a creative story using the title: An Adventure with the Easter Bunny. Place a peppermint candy treat in the egg for the student to eat.

Different messages may be used and changed daily.

Hide the eggs and instruct the students to go on a "Treasure Hunt" to find a special egg.

Arrange a bulletin board with a bunny theme for displaying the stories.

JUST FOR FUN

Provide drawing paper and crayons for
students to use to make a decorated
Easter egg. Using scissors, cut across
the egg as if it is cracked. Put the egg
back together with a brass fastener to
enable the egg to open and close. A
chick may be drawn and glued inside.

Use construction paper to make a
tree and branches to mount on a
bulletin board, and ask the students
to make decorated eggs to put on
the tree, or

Paint a bare tree branch white and provide egg shells (from which
the eggs have been blown)   for the students to
paint with pastel colors,   fill with small
artificial flowers   and hang by ribbons
from the   branches.

Provide art materials to enable
the students to:

   (1) Weave construction paper
        baskets

   (2) Make paper mache baskets

   (3) Make crepe paper covered
        baskets from frozen food
        or cottage cheese boxes.

The Easter Bunny may fill them!

The students will enjoy using drawing paper and crayons to make
a "mod" Easter Bunny.

write a story
two trees
what do you think
and illustrate it
what would
Display Stories Here
One day I was walking
What do you think about a tree...
Tree Talk
art
On the barren plains of Nebraska in 1872 Arbor Day had its beginning. Due to the dreams of one man, tree planting now takes place all over the United States on this holiday.

Ring Count
how old is the tree? Count the Rings
Shapely Silhouettes

Treasure Trees

CENTER PURPOSES:

> After completing this center, the student should develop understanding of Arbor Day through learning experiences in tree identification, writing dialogue, planting a tree, and computing a tree's age.

CENTER ACTIVITIES:

Communications

"Tree Talk"

Instruct the students to write a creative story using dialogue generated by one of the following ideas:

What would an apple tree say to a cherry tree?
What might two fir trees being cut for Christmas trees
    say to each other?
What advice could a tall oak tree give to a tree that
    has just been planted?
What might two trees say during a terrible storm?
What do you think a beautiful maple tree in autumn
    would say to an evergreen tree?
What do two trees in a forest say to each other when
    they hear men cutting trees?

Creative Arts

"Shapely Silhouettes"

Plan and take a class field trip to look at the different shapes of trees. Provide drawing paper for the students to use to sketch the different tree shapes. After returning from the trip, lead a group discussion concerning the different tree shapes observed. Place black construction paper in the center. Instruct the students to use the sketches as guides to make black tree shape silhouettes. Arrange the silhouettes on a bulletin board.

Environmental Studies

"Dig It"

Provide resource books and instruct the students to make
a list of good rules to follow when planting a tree. Following
these rules, provide a small tree and as a class project let
the students plant it on Arbor Day.

Quantitative Experience

"Ring Count"

On a chart mount a picture showing a cross section of a
tree, and print the following:

A tree's life story can be learned from the rings in
the trunk. A year's growth is one light and one dark
ring. Look at the picture of the cross section of the
tree and write and compute mathematical problems for
each question.

1. How old is the tree?
2. The year is 1974. What year was the tree planted?
3. If the tree had not been cut in 1974, how many
   more rings would it have had in 1998?
4. How much older or younger is the tree than you?
5. How many rings would two trees the same age have?
   Four trees?
6. Using the tree, write a mathematical problem for
   a friend to solve.
7. What kind of tree do you think this was? Draw a
   picture showing it.

Instruct the students to read and follow the directions printed
on the chart.

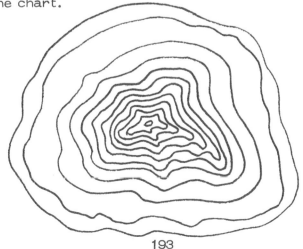

"Plot the Spot"

Print the following words
on strips of tagboard:

trunk
cambium layer
inner bark
outer bark
roots
sapwood
crown
heartwood

Instruct the students to place
the words on the correct spot
on the tree. A resource book
may be needed for this activity.

JUST FOR FUN

Provide art supplies to enable the
students to illustrate different ways
man uses trees.

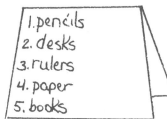

Ask the students to make a list of all
the objects in their classrooms that
come from trees. Print the list on
a chart and illustrate it to be displayed
in a conspicuous place in the classroom.

The students will enjoy writing
poetry about trees. The poems
can be illustrated and made into
a booklet and placed in the reading
corner or library.

Play a statue game. Ask the
students to pretend they are
trees moving in the wind. Provide
a record and instruct students to
move with the music. Stop the
record at different intervals and
observe the interesting statues
made by the student "trees".

Provide resource books for the
students to use to research the
origin of Arbor Day. Ask them
to write two or three paragraphs
about the significance of Arbor
Day and the different ways it has
been observed through the years.

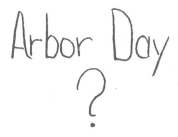

See how original students can be by pretending they are a newly
identified tree. Ask them to describe themselves as to how they
look, how big they are, where they grow, and how useful they
will be. Provide time for students to illustrate, share, and display
the creative stories.

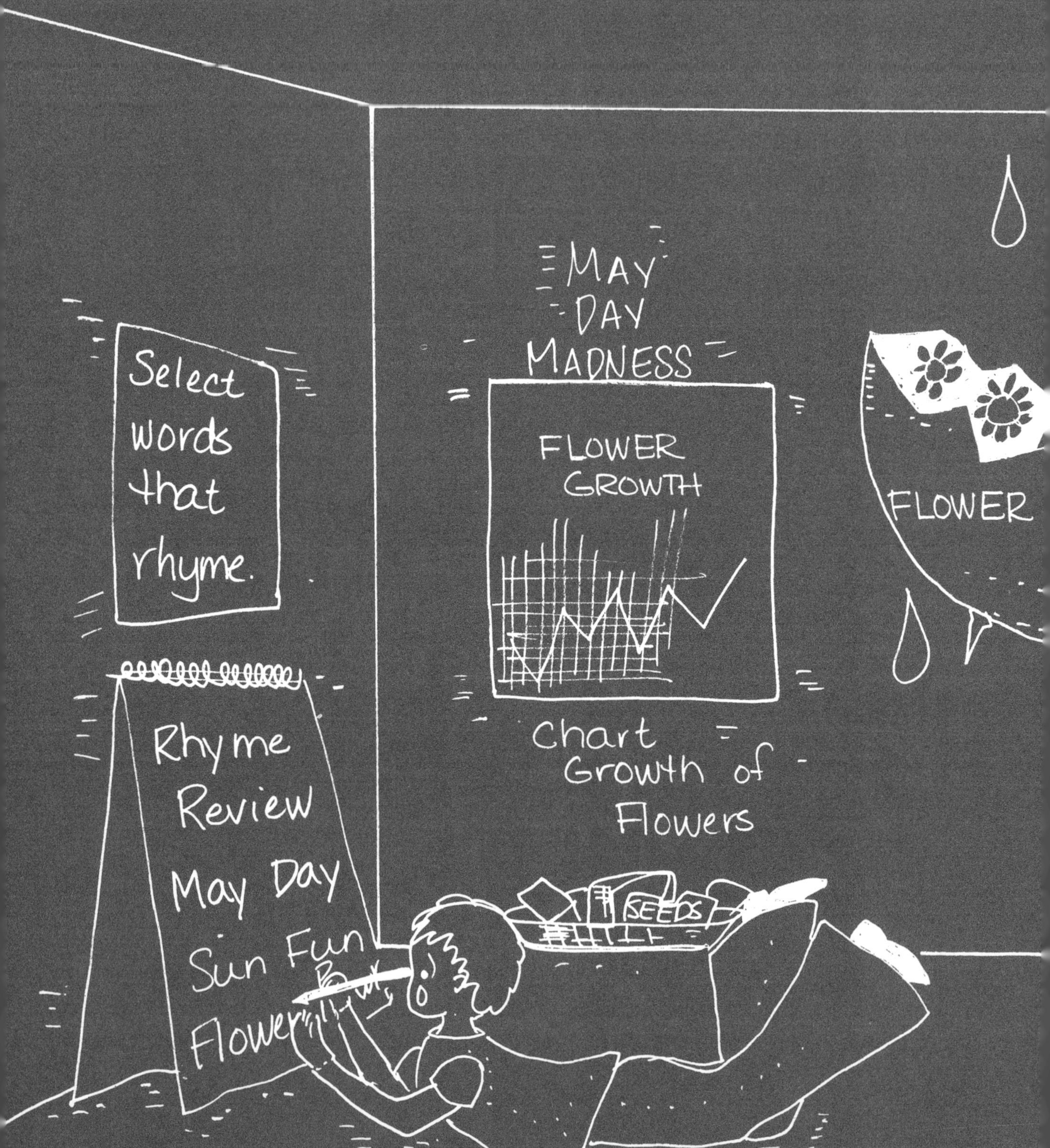
Select words that rhyme.
MAY DAY MADNESS
FLOWER GROWTH
FLOWER
Rhyme Review
May Day
Sun Fun
Flower
Chart Growth of Flowers
SEEDS

FLOWER

MAY MYSTERY

FLOWER FAIR

Identify the flowers

The first day of May is traditionally known as May Day. One May Day custom is secretly hanging a basket of flowers on a door to surprise a friend.

CENTER PURPOSES:

After completing this center, the
student should develop appreciation
for May Day through learning
experiences in paper construction,
mental imagery, flower identification
and charting growth time.

CENTER ACTIVITIES:

Communications

"Rhyme Review"

Instruct the students to select words that are connected with
May and its happenings and add a rhyming word.

Example: May Day
                Flower Power
                Sun Fun

The rhymes may be printed on a chart, illustrated and displayed
in a prominent spot in the classroom. They will then make
excellent titles or first lines for original poems.

Creative Arts

"May Mystery"

Provide construction paper, tissue paper, florist tape, wire
or pipe cleaners, and scissors for students to use to make
flowers. Instruct the students to arrange flowers in a bouquet
and hang a bouquet on every classroom door in the school.
The students may wish to enclose a card that reads "Guess who
wishes you a Happy May Day?"

Environmental Studies

"Flower Fair"

Display real, artificial or picture flowers on a large bulletin
board. Number each flower and ask the students to identify
as many flowers as they can. Provide resource books for
identification of unknown flowers. As a follow-up activity,
the students may wish to prepare displays of their own for
their classmates to identify.

Quantitative Experience

"May Day Madness"

Provide seed packets and instruct the students to compute
the length of the growing season necessary for the selected
flowers. Ask them to find the flowers that require the longest
and shortest growing seasons and make a chart showing the
differences.

"May Mix-up"

These flowers were planted by a confused farmer. Can you
unscramble them so everyone will know what they are. Draw
the picture beside the word.

s a i y d   d _ _ _ _

p l u i t   t _ _ _ _

t e l v i o   v _ _ _ _ _

o s r e   r _ _ _

s p a n y   p _ _ _ _

y l l i   l _ _ _

l i d d o f f a   d _ _ _ _ _ _ _

n i z n i a   z _ _ _ _ _

d r a i m l o g   m _ _ _ _ _ _ _

t a n i p e u   p _ _ _ _ _ _

l a d d i n n o e   d _ _ _ _ _ _ _ _ (oops!)

JUST FOR FUN

Since May 1 is a day of surprises, help the students to surprise each other. On strips of tagboard write every student's name; then ask each student to draw a name. Everyone is then to devise a special surprise to be found in the desk of their secret pal on May 1.

Provide resource books for the students to use to discover the origin of May Day. It will be interesting to find out if other countries celebrate May Day, and if so, how it is celebrated.

Plan and present a short program for parents or for another class. Some students may wish to read some poetry they have written, and others may wish to do the May Pole Dance.

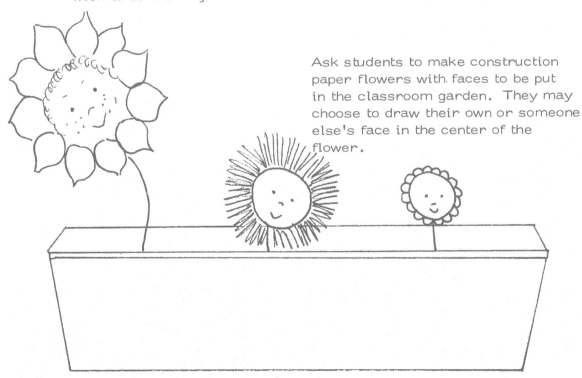

Ask students to make construction paper flowers with faces to be put in the classroom garden. They may choose to draw their own or someone else's face in the center of the flower.

work
here
display
Miles of Smiles
A day with Mother
A
day
with
mom
make a mobile
magazines
use old magazines.

Marvelous Moms

CENTER PURPOSES:

> After completing this center, the student should be able to express appreciation for Mother's Day through learning experiences in corsage-making, creative writing, recognizing Mother's chores, and time schedules.

CENTER ACTIVITIES:

Communications

"Miles of Smiles"

Instruct the students to write one or more paragraphs focusing on "How I Can Keep Mother Smiling..."

Ask them to draw pictures of their happy moms to illustrate the paragraphs.

Creative Arts

"A Day with Mother"

Provide a large collection of old magazines. Ask the students to look through the magazines to find pictures of major activities their mothers engage in during the day. These pictures may be cut out in various shapes, pasted to cardboard and hung from sewing thread or thin wire attached to a coat hanger to form a hanging mobile. Or, they could be used to cover a sturdy gift box (collage style) to be presented as a Mother's Day gift.

Environmental Studies

"Busy Moms"

Draw a large picture of a mother and display it in the center of a large sheet of mural paper pinned to a bulletin board. Instruct each student to use tempera paints to add a picture of a job that his mother does to the mural. After the mural is completed, students might wish to pantomime the jobs they illustrated and call on other students to go to the mural and point to the job being pantomimed.

Quantitative Experience

"Timetable Tally"

Ask each student to make a schedule of his mother's day. Instruct him to compute how many minutes she spends each day doing the various activities the student has listed, and to compute the total amount of time spent each week on these activities.

"Smiles and Frowns"

Preparation Directions:

1. Enlarge the game board below on tagboard.

2. Cut forty tagboard strips and on each strip write either a way to help Mother or to hinder her.

   Example: Set the table   Late for game, forgot
                                                      the garbage

3. Supply game markers for two players.

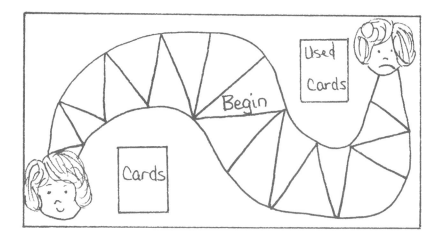

Player Directions:

1. The cards are shuffled and placed face down in a stack.

2. The first player draws a card, and if the item on the card helps Mother he moves toward the smile; if it hinders her he moves toward the frown.

3. Turns are taken until one player reaches the happy Mother and wins the game.

JUST FOR FUN

Provide blue ribbons, foil, and construction paper for the students to use to make a "blue ribbon" for the greatest mom.

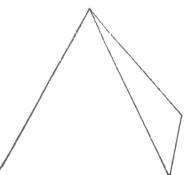

Instruct the students to make a tetrahedron and cover it with a collage of words that describe their mother. Shellac the finished tetrahedron to preserve it.

Ask the students to write a paragraph telling why they appreciate their mothers and how they could express this appreciation to their mothers. Provide ribbon, artificial flowers, tissue paper, glitter and pipe cleaners for the students to use to make corsages for their mothers.

Bring some records about mothers to the classroom and take time out for a "sing-along".

Ask the students to look through reference books to find accounts of the influence of mothers on some of the world's great people.

PickI
Pus
Display ads here
Try me
Pickles on Parade
introducing an exciting new pickle !!
...advertising is fun .... try advertising a pickle...
Pickle Productic
...design a factory
Pickle Factory
Pickle Week is celebrated during the month of May. Can you think of a better time to bring some extra laughter and humor into the classroom with an old-fashioned celebration?

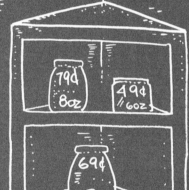

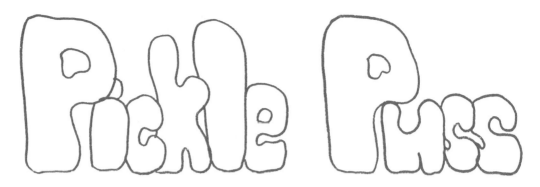

CENTER PURPOSES:

> After completing this center, the student should develop awareness of pickles as a part of the economic environment through learning experiences in cardboard box construction, advertising, job recognition, and problem solving.

CENTER ACTIVITIES:

Communications

"Pickles on Parade"

Ask the students to imagine a brand new pickle that has just been produced, and to think of a unique way of advertising this pickle. Have them enter their "ad" in a contest.

The prize? A jar of pickles!

Creative Arts

"Pickle Production"

Provide shoe boxes and art materials for the students to use to make a model of a pickle factory. Instruct them to carefully design the outside and inside, create a name for the company, and make a billboard for the factory's roof! (They may need to use resource books to gather information before beginning the construction.)

Environmental Studies

"Pickle Pickers"

Guide the students in listing all the people necessary for the entire process of pickle production. After the list is complete, provide art supplies for each student to use to draw one pickle worker. Using mural paper pinned to a bulletin board, assist the students in mounting their workers to represent the entire pickle production process.

Quantitative Experience

"Nickel for a Pickle"

In a corner of the center set up a small grocery shelf with pickle jars labeled with prices and weight. Instruct the students to compute the most expensive jar of pickles and least expensive jar according to the price per ounce.

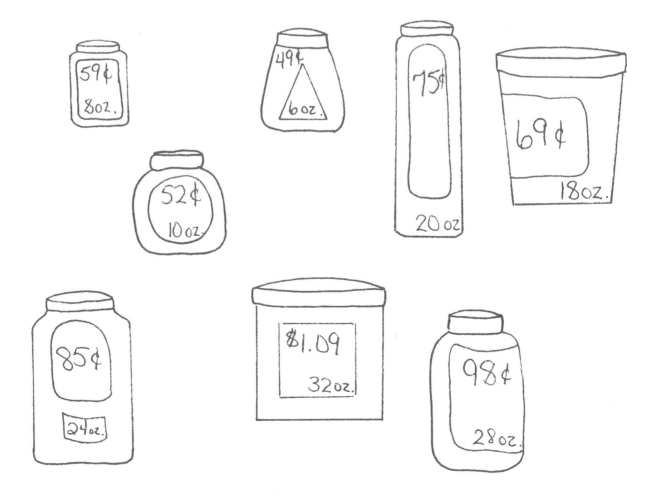

"Pickle Patch"

Preparation Directions:

1. Enlarge the game board below.
2. Make three markers in the shape of a cucumber.
3. Use a small square wooden block to make a die.
4. Print the following directions on four cards:

    Lose one turn   Move ahead one space
    Take another turn   Move back one space

Player Directions:

1. Each player selects a marker.
2. Place the cards in the center of the game board.
3. One player rolls the die and moves the correct number
    of spaces. When a player rolls an even number, he
    draws a card and follows the directions. The game
    continues until one player becomes a pickle and lands
    in the jar!

JUST FOR FUN

Instruct the students to list as many different kinds of pickles as they can and write a paragraph about the personality of one kind of pickle (sweet, dill, garlic, chips, relish, etc.).

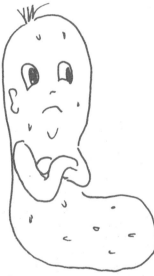

Display a "large" jar of chip pickles on a desk. Let the students guess the number of pickles in the jar. The student who comes the closest takes the jar of pickles.

Instruct the students to write a make-believe story about the origin of pickles. Provide resource books to be used to discover the real origin.

Ask the students to write a story about "The Life and Times of A Pickle Tester".

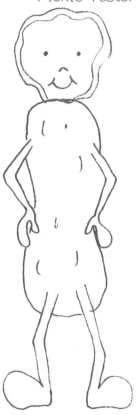

Provide many colors of construction paper, scissors, paste and magic markers. Ask the students to design "pickle people", complete with facial features, clothes, etc. They may be used to make a border for a chalk board or bulletin board.

Appoint a student committee to take a classroom poll to discover the students' favorite kind of pickle.

Invent recipes for pickle sundaes!

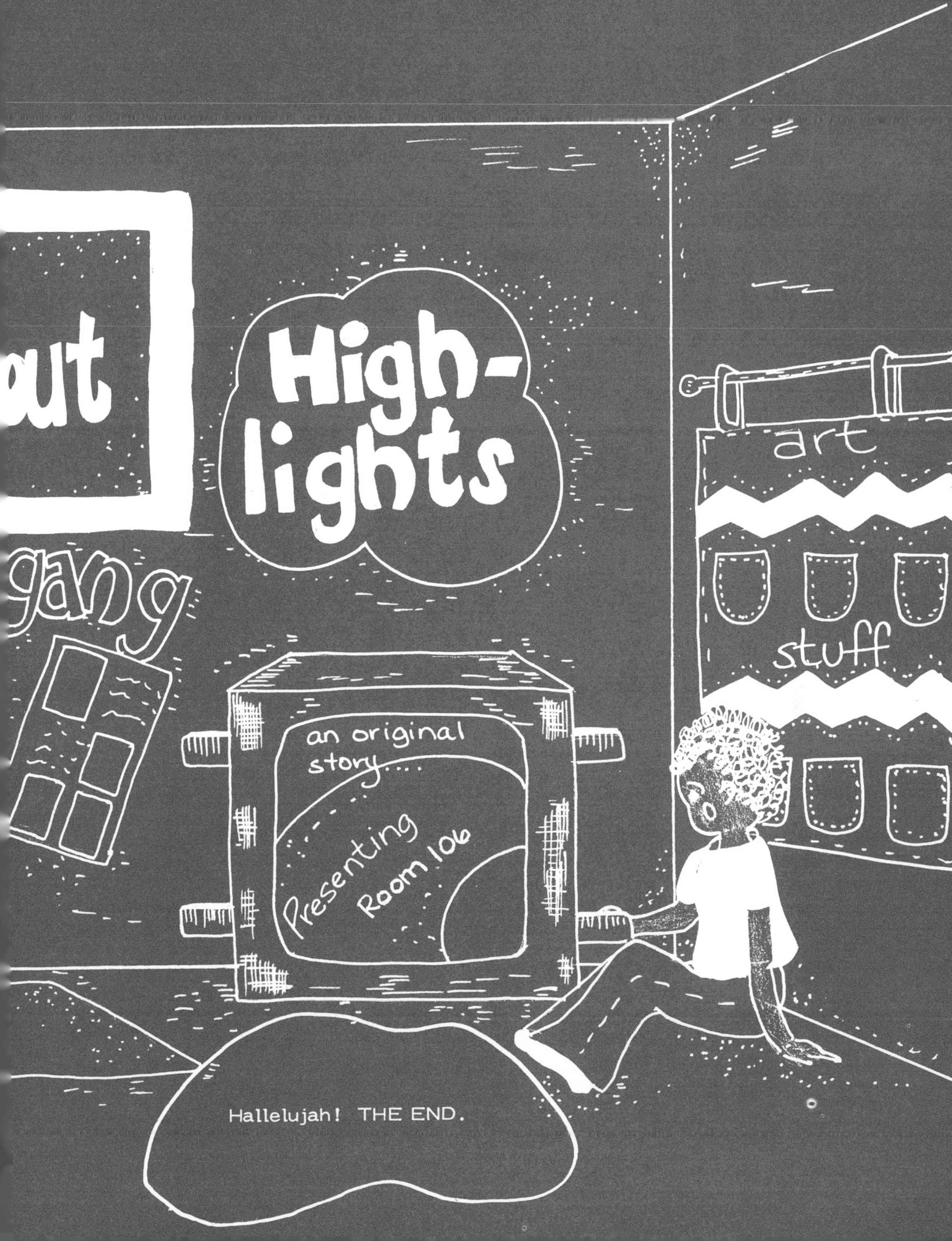

Hallelujah! THE END.

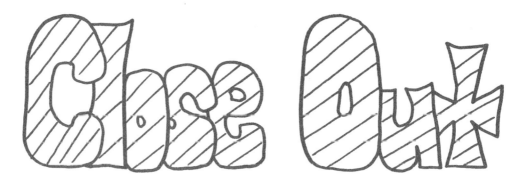

CENTER PURPOSES:

After completing this center, the student should develop appreciation for the special uniqueness of the last day of school, through learning experiences in making dioramas, compiling a class yearbook, creating a television program, and reviewing mathematical concepts.

CENTER ACTIVITIES:

Communications

"Our Gang"

Prepare work sheets by dividing sheets of paper into four equal boxes. Share several class or school yearbooks with the students, pointing out the qualities that make some yearbooks more attractive than others. Instruct the students to draw a self-portrait and write a few sentences about themselves. Remind them to proofread their material very carefully to make sure that it is worthy of inclusion in their own class yearbook. Class elected editors may then oversee the transfer of this material to duplication masters that have been divided into four equal parts. As the culminating activity each student will enjoy compiling and arranging the "printed" sheets and designing title pages and covers to make his own yearbook.

Creative Arts

"Bird's Eye View"

Lead a class discussion planned to help the students review the school year. Provide cardboard boxes and the necessary art materials for making dioramas showing special events or activities that have occurred during the school year. The students will want to include themselves and possibly some friends in their dioramas. Provide time for sharing and displaying the dioramas.

Environmental Studies

"Highlights"

Divide a long roll of shelf paper into equal sections and provide crayons, scissors, tape, and paste. Through class discussion plan a television program "featuring" the highlights of the school year. Use a cardboard box for the television set. Mount the roll of shelf paper on two dowels; anchor the dowels in holes cut in each side of the box and cut a square in the front to depict the screen. When this preparation has been completed, the students will enjoy drawing pictures of events of the school year that they remember as being very special and pasting or taping them to the roll of shelf paper. An accompanying script may be taped and time provided for the students to share the completed presentation in a group setting.

Quantitative Experience

"Fun and Facts"

Engage the students in a review of the different math concepts studied during the school year. Provide a brightly decorated box filled with 3 x 5 index cards. Instruct the students to work in pairs to prepare "problem cards" by writing the math problem on each side of the cards. After the "problem cards" have been replaced in the box, the same teams may work together, drawing one card at a time from the box and competing to recopy the problem and supply the correct answer first.

"Guess Who"

Preparation Directions:

1. Use two index cards for each student. Print a student's name on one card and print a clue about the student on the other.

2. Two or three players may play this game.

Player Directions:

1. Shuffle the cards and deal five cards to each player. Place the remaining cards in a stack in the middle of the table.

2. The first player asks for either a card with a student's name or a clue card. If the other player does not have the card, the player must draw a card from the stack. Two matching cards make a "book".

3. The game continues until one player disposes of all his cards and wins the game.

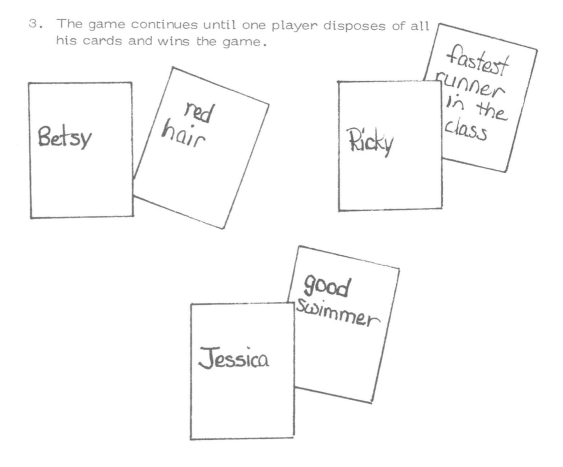

JUST FOR FUN

Provide art supplies to enable the
students to paint a mural illustrating
events of the school year.

Plan and present an original
play entitled "The Year That
Was". Encourage all the
students to make contributions
to the script by writing lines
related to the highlights of the
year as they recall them.

Instruct the students to write a creative story about one of the
following ideas:

(1) Write a letter telling your desk goodbye.

(2) How the classroom feels after everyone leaves for
     summer vacation.

(3) What the pencil sharpener said as the last pencil was
     sharpened.

(4) The most exciting hour during the school year.

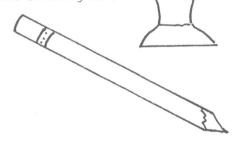

Ask the students to write a letter
or make a card for the custodial
personnel thanking them for
making the school atmosphere
more pleasant during the year.

The students will enjoy writing
secret goodbye notes and hiding
them in their classmates' desks.

invent a new factory
Design a flag and share it with a friend
art
stuff
CTORY
answer the questions inside
Flag Designers

 and

CENTER PURPOSES:

After completing this center, the student should develop understanding of Flag Day and flags through learning experiences in designing a class flag, creating alphabet flags, displaying a flag, and using numerical computation skills.

CENTER ACTIVITIES:

Communications

"Talking Flags"

Using a resource book as a guide, prepare the International Alphabet Flags on a piece of tagboard and place them in the center. Discuss the use and importance of the International Alphabet Flags and use the prepared flags to send messages. Provide construction paper, scissors and crayons to enable the students to make their own alphabet flags. They will then enjoy exchanging messages using their uniquely created alphabet flags.

Creative Arts

"Flag Designers"

Lead a group discussion about the many kinds of flags. Explain that there are flags to represent countries, presidents, kings, queens, states, cities, Boy Scouts, Red Cross, and other organizations and ideas. Provide art supplies for the students to use to design and make a class flag. Provide time for sharing the flags and appoint a student committee to arrange them creatively on a bulletin board.

Environmental Studies

"Flag Wavers"

Provide encyclopedia and other resource books and arrange time
for the students to read why Flag Day is celebrated. Lead a
class discussion and make a list of various ways to display a
flag. The list might include the following:

From a building	Marching
Over a street	Behind a speaker
At half mast	On a platform
With other flags	On a casket
Upside down	On a car

Instruct the students to make posters illustrating three ways a
flag can be displayed. Take students outside and demonstrate
the correct way to raise and lower a flag.

Quantitative Experience

"Flag Factories"

Many people are involved in various jobs in the manufacture of
flags. Fabrics must be purchased, flags must be sold, employees
paid, and a profit is hopefully made. Print the following directions
on a piece of tagboard and place in the center.

You have just opened a flag factory.
Read the following directions and answer or complete each
question.

1. Give your factory a name.
2. Design a sign for your factory.
3. Write an advertisement for your factory.
4. How many employees will you have?
5. How much money will each employee be paid per hour?
6. Each employee will work eight hours per day. How much
   money will each employee earn in one day? How much
   money will each employee earn in one week?
7. How much money will all the employees earn in one day?
   How much money will all the employees earn in one week?
8. Your factory makes small flags, thirty-six inches in width
   and thirty-six inches in length. You can make one flag from
   one yard of material. How much fabric will you need if you
   make twenty-five flags each day? How much fabric will you
   need for one week?
9. Each flag sells for $4.95. You sell twenty-five flags each day.
   How much money will you make in one day? How much will you
   make in one week?
10. Did you make any profit? Prove your answer.

"Pennant Play"

Preparation Directions:

1. Using an encyclopedia or other resource book, make the International Numeral Pennants on tagboard and place in the center.
2. On twenty index cards make two sets of the International Numeral Pennants. The pennants must be the correct color.
3. On twenty index cards make two sets of numerals from zero to nine.
4. Two players may play this game.

Player Directions:

1. The cards are shuffled and five cards are dealt to each player. The remaining cards are placed between the players.
2. The first player asks his opponent for either a pennant or a numeral card. If the opponent has the card he must give it to him and the first player gets another turn. A matching pennant card and a numeral card form a book and are placed in the middle. If his opponent does not have the card, the player draws a card from the stack.
3. The game continues until one player runs out of cards. The player with the most books wins.

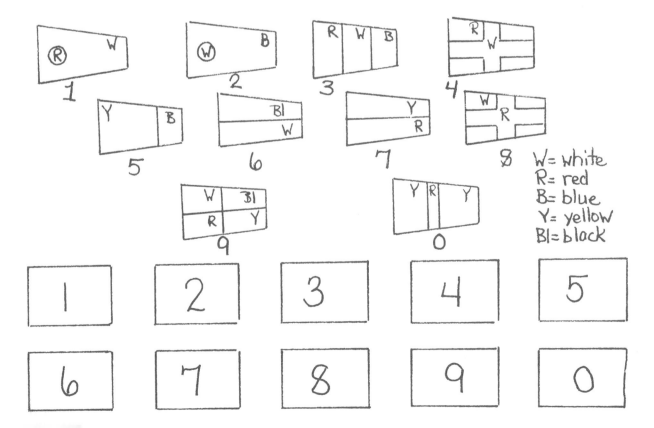

JUST FOR FUN

Provide a time for the class
to go outside and sit where they can see
the flag. Let students write a poem
about the flag. Share and display the
poetry.

The astronauts have just
landed on Mars. Design
the flag they may have found
there.

Write a creative story using one of the following ideas:

A strange flag was flying...
The battle was almost over when the pirate's flag was.
When Betsy Ross completed the first American flag...

Provide mural paper, tempera paint
and crayons to be used to make a
mural of all the flags of the United
Nations.

Bring several records of songs
written about the flag to class.
Provide time for a sing-along.

Ask the students to use the title "What My Flag Means To Me" to
write and illustrate an essay. Compile the completed essays into
a class booklet to be placed in the reading corner for all to enjoy.
Appoint a committee to make a cover and table of contents for the
booklet.

Pops are
cozy corner
Job Market
crossword puzzle
Pops
Stat
age
Father's Day
is the third Sunday in
June.
Give Father an extra thank-you
for all he does.

Pops are Tops

CENTER PURPOSES:

> After completing this center, the student should be able to express appreciation for Father's Day through learning experiences in art, using descriptive words, occupations, and averages.

CENTER ACTIVITIES:

Communications

"Dad Diorama"

Instruct the students to make a word diorama on a strip of construction paper 6" x 24". The paper should be folded to form four 6" x 4" rectangles. At the bottom of each rectangle the student must think up a word beginning with "F" that describes their father. Above each word they may illustrate how this describes their father.

Creative Arts

"Fathers Unlimited"

Plan a group "sharing time" designed to allow each student to share the things that he feels are "extra special" about his father. (Suggest that students without fathers select a male in their lives that they would like to honor.) Provide 9" x 12" sheets of white construction paper and colored chalk. Ask the students to draw portraits of their fathers designed to feature special hobbies, occupations or interests. (For example, one father might wear fishing clothes, one a welder's helmet, one might be seated at an executive desk, one in a courtroom, another behind the wheel of a truck, etc.) The portraits may be framed in black construction paper and mounted on a bulletin board entitled "Fathers Unlimited".

Environmental Studies

"Job Market"

Ask each student to write a three-paragraph description of his father's occupation. Reference books should be provided for tracing the history, social importance, etc. of the occupations. Provide special paper for re-copying the completely corrected papers to be bound into a book for the classroom reading corner.

Quantitative Experience

"Vital Statistics"

Instruct the students to work in small groups to find the average weight, height and ages of their fathers. When all group work is completed, assist the class in working as a total group to find the "average" father for the entire class.

"Job Market"

If you can solve their riddles, you'll be able to fill in the puzzle,
and see what all these men do.

Across:

1. I fill prescriptions.
2. I deliver quarts and pints.
5. My office is an airplane.
7. I help design buildings.
10. I help people save their money.
11. I'm a great cook.
12. I work in a shop with a
    red and white pole.

Down:

1. I help keep law and order.
2. I might play in an orchestra.
3. Mechanical, electrical or
   chemical might be part of
   my title.
4. I help keep you healthy.
6. My busy day is Sunday.
8. I go to school every day.
9. I spend a lot of time in court.

JUST FOR FUN

Provide art supplies for the
students to make their fathers'
favorite hat. The hats could
illustrate an occupation, hobby
or special sports interest.

The students may make a
pencil holder for their
fathers by covering a small
juice can with popsicle sticks,
macaroni, string, buttons,
paper mache or beans and
seeds. The cans may be
painted or shellacked after
the glue is dry.

Fathers whose jobs or hobbies would
be of interest to the group might be
invited to come to the classroom to
talk about their jobs or hobbies.

The boys might enjoy projecting into the future and drawing their
pictures when they are fathers. The girls could draw pictures of
the kind of father they would like for their children.

Make a bulletin board entitled
"Perfect Pops". Ask the students
to bring a picture of their fathers
to mount on the board.

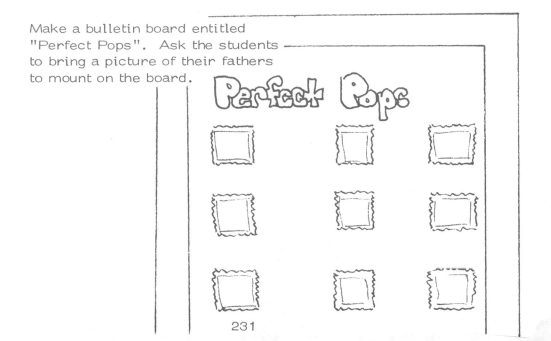

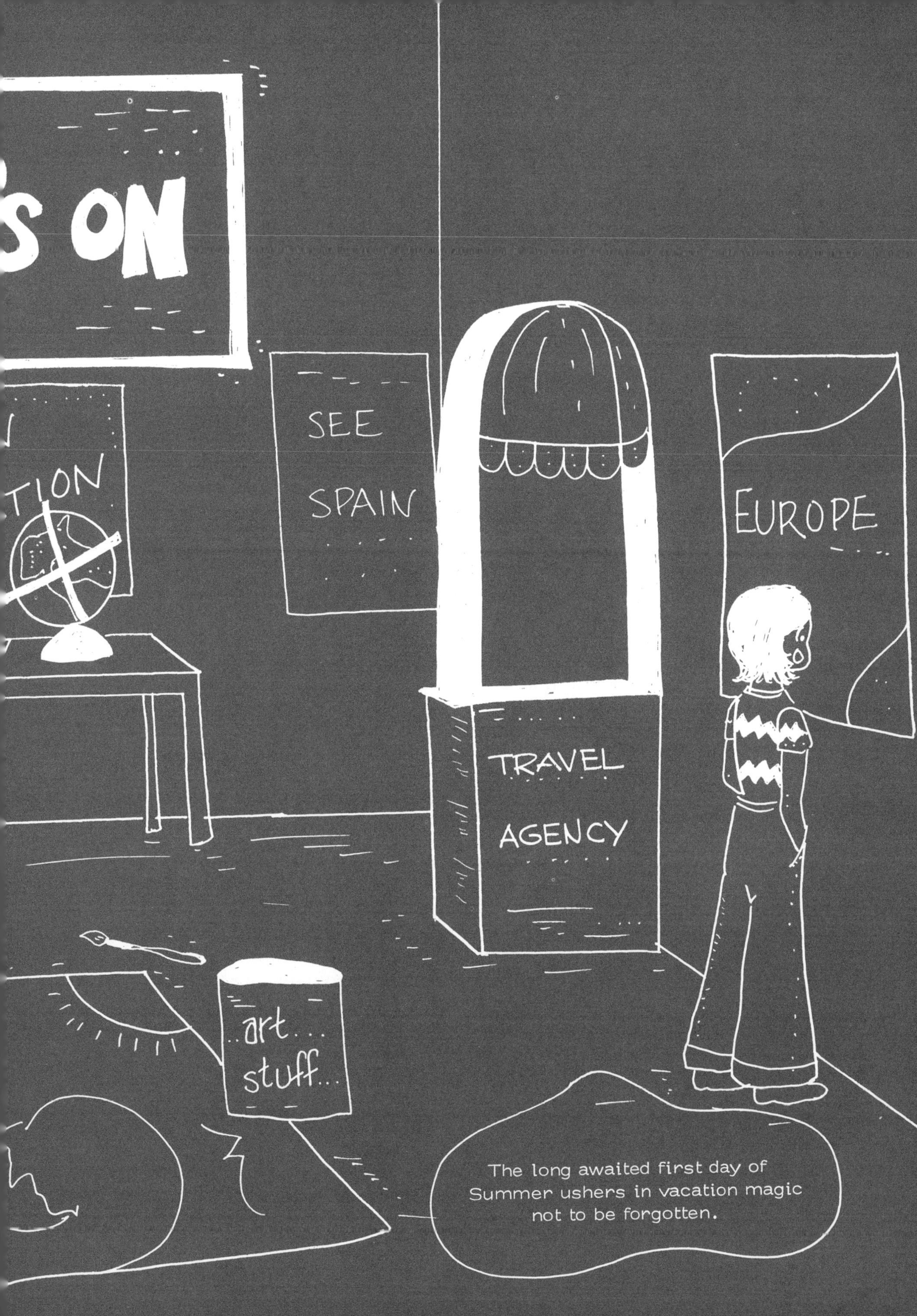

SEE SPAIN
EUROPE
TRAVEL AGENCY
art... stuff...
The long awaited first day of Summer ushers in vacation magic not to be forgotten.

CENTER PURPOSES:

> After completing this center, the student should be able to express appreciation for the first day of Summer through learning experiences in writing travel reports, creating underwater scenes, investigating climatic conditions, and using common measurements.

CENTER ACTIVITIES:

Communications

"Travel Bureau"

Instruct the students to select a place they may go on their vacation or would like to go. Ask them to use resource books to gain information as background to use in writing a report about this city or resort, what there is to see there, where it is located, and how they will get there. Illustrations will make the reports more interesting.

Creative Arts

"Big Dip"

Provide white construction paper, crayons, blue water colors, and paint brushes. Instruct the students to use crayons to draw an underwater scene omitting the water. When the picture is finished they may use blue water colors to paint over the entire scene to create the water.

Seaweed, small shells and stones, and other relevent objects may be pasted on to give a three dimensional effect.

Environmental Studies

"Nation Location"

Provide resource books and instruct the students to locate
a city in the southern and eastern hemispheres with a
climate similar to their city's climate. Have them list the
factors that influence the climate of their own and the other
two cities.

Miami, Florida
Iquitos, Peru
Granada, Spain

Quantitative Experience

"Heat Wave"

To keep cool, instruct the students in the center to prepare some
"Kool Aid" to be served later in the day. Provide measuring
spoons and cups and a gallon container. Students will need to
read the instructions and find how much water, "Kool Aid",
sugar and ice will be needed to serve all the members of their
class.

"Vacation Travels"

Preparation Directions:

1. Enlarge the map below on tagboard.

2. Write the names of a well-known city or resort on thirty tagboard strips to be used as game cards.

3. Cut thirty small square markers from construction paper. Make half of them red and the other half blue.

4. Two players may play this game.

Player Directions:

1. The deck of cards is shuffled and placed face down in a stack.

2. The first player draws a card and reads the name of the city or resort. If he can tell which state it is in, he may place a marker on the state; if he misses, he waits until his next turn.

3. Players take turns until one player has marked twelve states and wins the game.

JUST FOR FUN

Make pictures of the beach and shore more realistic by gluing sand in place to represent the beach.

Provide students with a list of books that they might enjoy reading during the Summer.

Motivate some creative writing with the following topics:

- It was the middle of Summer and each day got colder and colder...
- All swimming pools had been drained. Where had the water gone...
- We were on vacation and I got lost in the city...
- Swimming in the ocean, I bumped into a whale...
- Our baseball team was playing for the championship and the bats were gone...
- We opened a babysitting agency one summer, and did we have problems...

Ask the students to select one hobby and write an account of how they could pursue this hobby during the summer.

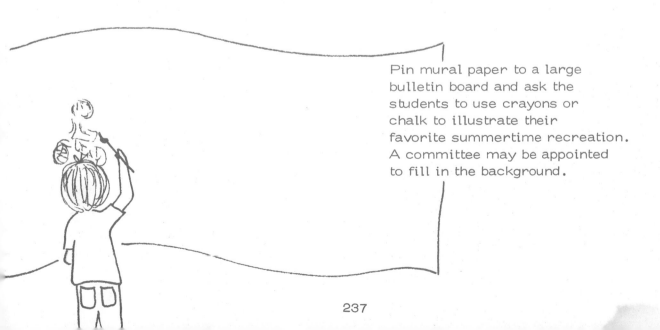

Pin mural paper to a large bulletin board and ask the students to use crayons or chalk to illustrate their favorite summertime recreation. A committee may be appointed to fill in the background.

The Fourth of July is a legal holiday commemorating the birth of our nation. Over the years picnics, fireworks, and parades have marked this holiday in a uniquely American way.

Real
Researchers

1. Independence
   Hall

2. thomas
   Jefferson

3. John Hancock

PLAN A 4th of
JULY PICNIC

the
Gazette

Chicken
$1.29

lemonade
20¢

CENTER PURPOSES:

> After completing this center, the student should develop appreciation and understanding of the Fourth of July through learning experiences in writing poetry, doing research and giving an oral report, counting money, and art.

CENTER ACTIVITIES:

Communications

"Patriotic Poets"

To provide student motivation, read some poetry and discuss various rhyming patterns. Print the following words on strips of tagboard and place in an attractively covered box:

freedom	lemonade	holiday
firecracker	watermelon	independence
sparkler	parade	July 4
picnic	flag	birthday

Instruct the students to close their eyes, take one idea from the box, and write a poem containing four lines, two of which rhyme. Encourage the students to spend as much time in this center as they wish.

Creative Arts

"Fancy Fireworks"

Fireworks have always been associated with the Fourth of July. By leading a class discussion, help students to understand that fireworks can be dangerous and that many cities have passed laws forbidding the sale of fireworks. Some cities have hired trained workmen to explode fireworks at special Fourth of July celebrations. Fireworks are fun and exciting to watch.

Provide drawing paper, brightly colored tempera paints, and drinking straws. Instruct the students to create colorful and exciting make-believe fireworks by dipping the straw in paint and gently blowing the paint-filled straw on the paper. Display the make-believe fireworks attractively on a bulletin board.

Environmental Studies

"Real Researchers"

Lead a group discussion planned to enable the students to understand the importance of the Fourth of July. Divide the class into five groups. Provide resource books and instruct each group to select one of the following ideas to be used as the theme of an oral report.

> Independence Hall
> Declaration of Independence
> Continental Congress
> Thomas Jefferson
> John Hancock
> Thirteen Colonies

The groups may prepare charts, posters or to make the reports more interesting.

Quantitative Experience

"Pack Your Basket"

Everyone likes a Fourth of July picnic. Place the food advertisements from the daily newspaper in the center. Instruct the students to plan a picnic menu, look at the food advertisements, and make a shopping list. Ask them to itemize the prices and compute the total amount of money needed to buy the food.

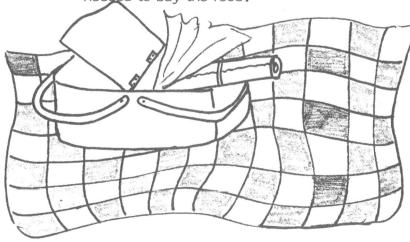

"Passing Parade"

Preparation Directions:

1. Enlarge the game board below on tagboard.
2. Using strips of tagboard, write the following phrases:

You're thirsty. Stop at the lemonade stand. Move ahead one space.

The band begins to play. Move ahead one space.

Wave at the spectators. Move ahead one space.

You're tired. Stop and rest. Lose one turn.

You're getting behind. Move ahead two spaces.

The clown fell. Move back one space.

You dropped your band instrument. Move back one space, but take another turn.

The floats are being judged. Move ahead one space.

The mayor is waving at you. Move ahead two spaces.

The photographer is taking pictures. Move ahead one space and take another turn.

The wind blows your hat off. Move ahead one space.

Here comes the rain! Move ahead two spaces, but lose one turn.

3. Provide three markers.

Player Directions:

1. Each player selects a marker and places it on the game board.
2. The cards are shuffled and placed face down. Taking turns, players draw a card and move the number of spaces indicated.
3. The first player to reach "finish" wins the game.

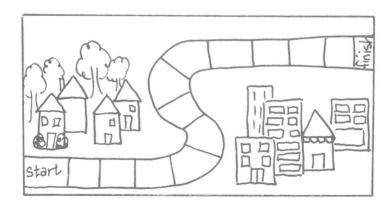

JUST FOR FUN

Plan and paint a mural depicting the
signing of the Declaration of
Independence. Display the mural
in the school hall for others to
enjoy.

Plan a Fourth of July class
parade. Ask each student to
represent an important person,
place, thing, or idea. Provide
art supplies for the students to
use to make simple costumes.
The parade route may include
other classrooms.

Encourage the students to become
more patriotic by providing art
supplies to enable them to make
patriotic posters and write
patriotic slogans.

Ask the students to use one of the
following ideas to write a creative
story:

   The firecracter who lost his
      bang

   The mystery of the missing
      picnic food

   The invisible parade

   The first fourth of July celebration

   July 4, 2001

notes

This is to certify that

_____

has completed one full unit of Special Day Learning Activities and is hereby awarded this Wreath of Achievement

October Fright

December Delights

February favorites

March
is Breezin' in

Magical May

ANSWERS FOR PUZZLES AND QUIZZES

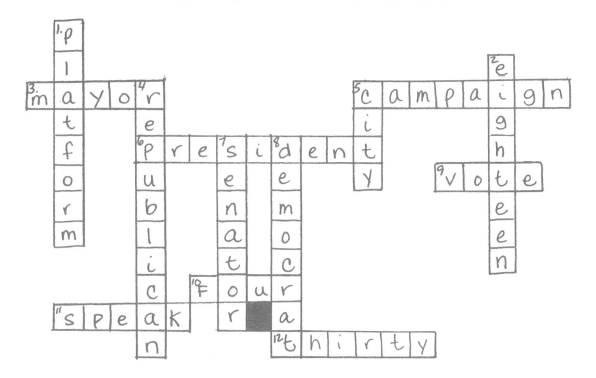

ELECTIONS – THE RACE IS ON – "Puzzle Power" (answers)

PUN WEEK – FUN PUNS – "Fun Finders" (answers)

1. golf
2. baseball
3. bowl
4. sailing
5. tennis

6. sewing
7. cooking
8. football
9. carpenter
10. plant

GEORGE WASHINGTON'S BIRTHDAY – WASHINGTON WRITE-UPS
"Mount Vernon Mystery" (answers)

VALENTINE'S DAY – HEARTY PARTY – "Secret Senders" (answers)

Alan	Sandy	Ed
Nan	Elaine	Ann
Ted	Linda	Dave

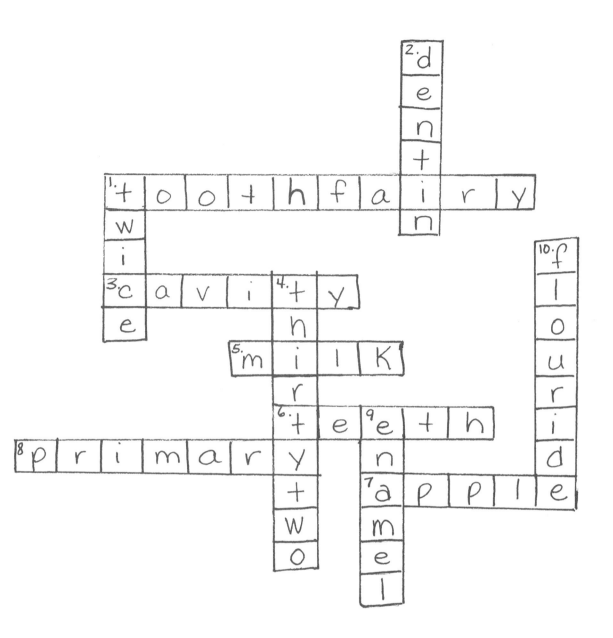

DENTAL HEALTH WEEK – THE BRUSH OFF – "Tooth Teasers"
(answers)

259

1. A l i
2. K i n g
3. A a r o n
4. C a r v e r
5. S i m p s o n
6. R o b i n s o n
7. A r m s t r o n g
8. W a s h i n g t o n
9. C h a m b e r l a i n
10. A l t h e a G i b s o n

BLACK HISTORY WEEK – PARADE OF HEROES – "Pyramid of Heroes"
(answers)

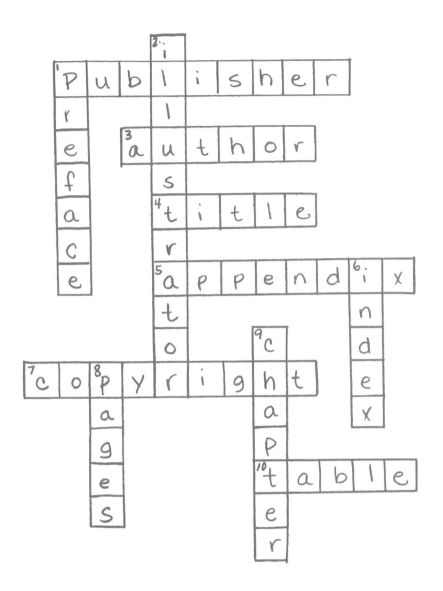

NATIONAL BOOK WEEK - IN A BIND - "All Parts Accounted For"
(answers)

MAY DAY - FLOWER SHOWER - "May Mix-up" (answers)

daisy		daffodil
tulip		zinnia
violet	lily	marigold
rose		petunia
pansy		dandelion

FATHER'S DAY – POPS ARE TOPS – "Job Market" (answers)

BOOKS FOR STUDENTS

First Day of School

Adelson, Leone, All Ready for School. N. Y.: McKay, 1957.

Amoss, Bertha, The Very Worst Thing. N.Y.: Parents Magazine Press, 1972.

Hall, Marie, Bad Boy, Good Boy. N. Y.: Crowell, 1967.

First Day of Autumn

Bancroft, Henrietta, Down Come the Leaves, New York: Crowell, 1961.

Banks, Marjorie Ann, How We Celebrate Our Fall Holidays, N. Y.: Benefic, 1964.

Caulfield, Peggy, Leaves. New York: Coward, 1962.

Fisher, Aileen, Now That Days Are Colder. New York: Bowman, 1973.

Fisher, Aileen, Where Does Everyone Go? New York: Crowell, 1961.

Fox, Charles P., When Autumn Comes. New York: Reilly & Lee, 1966.

Jacobs, L. B., Poetry for Autumn. Illinois: Garrard, 1968.

Kumin, Maxine W., Follow the Fall. New York: Putnam, 1961.

Lenski, Lois, Now It's Fall. New York: Walck, 1948.

Miles, Betty, A Day of Autumn. New York: Knopf, 1967.

Shapp, Charles and Martha, Let's Find Out About Fall. New York: Watts, 1963.

Tresselt, Alvin R., Autumn Harvest. New York: Lothrop, 1951.

Weygant, Sister Noemi, It's Autumn, Philadelphia: Westminister, 1968.

American Indian Day

Baldwin, Gordon, How Indians Really Lived. New York: Putnam, 1967.

Brewster, Benjamin, The First Book of Indians. New York: Watts, 1950.

Farquhar, Margaret, <u>Indian Children of America</u>. New York: Holt Rinehart & Winston, 1964.

Jones, Jane Clark, <u>The American Indian in America</u>, Vol. I and Vol. II. Minn.: <u>Lerner</u>, 1973.

Martini, Teri, <u>The True Book of Indians</u>. Chicago: Children's Press, 1954.

<u>Columbus Day</u>

Dalgliesh, Alice, <u>The Columbus Story</u>. N. Y.: Scribner's, 1955.

D'Aulaire, Ingir & Edgar, <u>Columbus</u>. New York: Doubleday, 1955.

DeKay, James T., <u>Meet Christopher Columbus</u>. New York: Random House, 1968.

Judson, Clara Ingram, <u>Christopher Columbus</u>. Chicago: Tollett, 1960.

Kaufman, Mervyn, <u>Christopher Columbus</u>. Ill.: Garrard, 1963.

McGovern, Ann, <u>The Story of Christopher Columbus</u>. New York: Random, 1962.

Showers, Paul, <u>Columbus Day</u>. New York: Crowell, 1965.

<u>Halloween</u>

Adams, Adrienne, <u>A Woggle of Witches</u>. New York: Scribner's, 1971.

Balian, Lorna, <u>Humbug Witch</u>. Nashville: Abingdon, 1965.

Barth, Edna, <u>Witches, Pumpkins, and Grinning Ghosts</u>. New York: Seabury Press, 1972.

Battles, Edith, <u>The Terrible Trick or Treat</u>. New York: Young Scott, 1970.

Benarde, Anita, <u>The Pumpkin Smasher</u>. New York: Walker & Co., 1972.

Borten, Helen, <u>Halloween</u>. New York: Crowell, 1965.

Bradbury, Ray, The Halloween Tree. New York: Knopf, 1972.

Bridwell, Norman, Clifford's Halloween. New York: Four Winds Press, 1966.

Bright, Robert, Georgie's Halloween. New York: Doubleday & Co., 1958.

Calhoun, Mary, The Witch of Hissing Hill. New York: Morrow, 1964.

Calhoun, Mary, Wobble the Witch Cat. New York: Morrow Co., 1958.

Carroll, Ruth, The Witch Kitten. New York: Walck, Inc., 1973.

Cooper, Paulette, Let's Find Out About Halloween. New York: Watts, 1972.

DeLage, Ida, The Old Witch Goes to the Ball. Illinois: Garrard, 1969.

Dietrich, Wilson, Powee's Jack-O-Lantern. Minn.: Denison Co., 1969.

Embry, Margaret, The Blue-Nosed Witch. New York: Holiday House, 1956.

Friedrich, Priscilla and Otto, The Marshmallow Ghosts. New York: Lothrop, Lee & Shepard Co., 1960.

Hays, Wilmer Pitchford, Highland Halloween. New York: Coward McCann, 1962.

Helmrath, Marilyn and Bartlett, Janet, Bobby Bear's Halloween. Minn.: Oddo Publ., 1968.

Hippel, Ursula von, The Craziest Halloween. New York: Coward McCann, Inc., 1957.

Kahane, Jacqueline, The Kitten in the Pumpkin Patch. New York: Warne & Co., 1973.

Laughlin, Florence, The Little Leftover Witch. New York: MacMillan Co., 1960.

Lewis, Mary, The Halloween Kangaroo. New York: Ives
    Washburn, 1964.

Mariana, Miss Flora McFlimsey's Halloween. New York:
    Lothrop, 1972.

Martin, Patricia Miles, The Pumpkin Patch. New York:
    Putnam's, 1966.

Miller, Edna, Mousekin's Golden House. New Jersey: Prentice-
    Hall, 1964.

Ott, John, Peter Pumpkin. New York: Doubleday, 1963.

Patterson, Lillie, Halloween. Illinois: Garrard Co., 1963.

Purdy, Susan, Suddenly – A Witch! New York: Lippincott Co., 1970.

Scott, Ann Herbert, Let's Catch A Monster. New York:
    Lothrop, 1969.

Sechrist, Elizabeth, Heigh-Ho for Halloween. Philadelphia:
    Macrae Smith Co., 1948.

Unwin, Nora, Proud Pumpkin. New York: Dutton, 1953.

Yolen, Jane, The Witch Who Wasn't. New York: MacMillan, 1964.

Fire Prevention Week

Tamarin, Alfred H., Fire Fighting in America. New York:
    MacMillan, 1971.

Zaffa, George J., Big Book of Real Fire Engines. New York:
    Grossett and Dunlap, 1958.

Election Day

Lindop, Edmund, The First Book of Elections. New York: Watts, 1968.

Phelan, Mary Kay, Election Day. New York: Crowell, 1967.

Schwartz, Alvin, The People's Choice. New York: Dutton Co., 1968.

Thanksgiving

Balion, Lorna, Sometimes It's Turkey, Sometimes It's Feathers. Nashville: Parthenon Press, 1973.

Barksdale, Lena, The First Thanksgiving. New York: Alfred A. Knoph, 1966.

Bartlett, Robert Merrill, Thanksgiving Day. New York: Thomas Y. Crowell, 1965.

Dalgliesh, Alice, The Thanksgiving Story. New York: Charles Scribner's Sons, 1954.

Devlin, Wende and Harry, Cranberry Thanksgiving. New York: Parents' Magazine Press, 1971.

Ellis, Mary Jackson, Gobble, Gobble, Gobble. Minnesota: T. S. Denison and Co., 1956.

Embry, Margaret, Peg-Leg Willy. New York: Holiday House, 1966.

Harper, Wilhelmina, The Harvest Feast. New York: E. P. Dutton & Co., Inc., 1965.

Hays, William Pitchford, Naughty Little Pilgrim. New York: Ives Washburn, Inc., 1969.

Hays, Wilma Pitchford, Pilgrim Thanksgiving. New York: Coward-McCann, Inc., 1955.

Hays, Wilma Pitchford, Pilgrims To The Rescue. New York: Ives Washburn, Inc., 1971.

Janice, Little Bear's Thanksgiving. New York: Lothrop, Lee & Shepard Co., Inc., 1967.

Luckhardt, Mildred Corell, Thanksgiving Feast and Festival. Nashville – New York: Abingdon Press, 1966.

Peterson, Bettina, Thanksgiving Is For What We Have. New York: Ives Washburn, Inc., 1959.

Kogers, Lori, The First Thanksgiving. Chicago: Follett Publishing Co., 1962.

Sechrist, Elizabeth Hough and Woolsey, Janette, It's Time for Thanksgiving. Philadelphia: Macrae Smith Co., 1957.

Shapp, Martha and Charles, Let's Find Out About Thanksgiving. New York: Franklin Watts, Inc., 1964.

Weisgard, Leonard, The Plymouth Thanksgiving. New York: Doubleday and Co., Inc., 1967.

Wyndham, Lee, A Holiday Book, Thanksgiving. Illinois: Garrard Publishing Co., 1963.

First Day of Winter

Adelson, Leone, All Ready for Winter. New York: McKay, 1952.

Anson, Brian, Gus and Gilly, The Winter Journey. New York: Dutton, 1970.

Baker, Laura N., Torkel's Winter Friend. New York: Hale, 1961.

Bancroft, Henrietta, Animals in Winter. New York: Crowell, 1963.

Barker, Will, Winter-Sleeping Wildlife. New York: Harper Row, 1958.

Chaffin, Lillie D., Bear Winter. New York: MacMillan, 1969.

Christian, Mary Blount, The First Sign of Winter. New York: Parents Magazine Press, 1973.

Fox, Charles Philip, When Winter Comes. New York: Reilly & Lee, 1962.

Hoff, Sydney, When Will It Snow? New York: Harper Row, 1971.

Jansson, Tove, Moominland Midwinter. New York: Walck, 1962.

Knotts, Howard, The Winter Cat. New York: Harper and Row, 1972.

Kumin, Maxine W., A Winter Friend. New York: Putnam, 1961.

Lenski, Lois, I Like Winter. New York: Walck, 1950.

Marino, Dorothy, Buzzy Bear's Winter Party. New York: Watts, 1967.

Marriott, Alice, Winter-Telling Stories. New York: Crowell, 1969.

Miles, Betty, A Day of Winter. New York: Knopf, 1961.

Russell, Helen R., Winter: A Field Trip Guide. New York:
    Little, 1972.

Sarasy, Phyllis, Winter Sleepers. New York: Prentice-Hall, 1962.

Shapp, Charles, and Martha, Let's Find Out About Winter. New
    York: Watts, 1963.

Shire, Ellen, The Snow Kings. New York: Walker & Co., 1969.

Weggant, Sister Noemi, It's Winter. Philadelphia: Westminster, 1969.

Hanukkah

Cedarbaum, Sophia N., Chanuko. New York: Union of American
    Hebrew Congregations, 1960.

Morrow, Betty and Louis Hartman, A Holiday Book, Jewish Holidays.
    Illinois: Garrard Publishing Co., 1967.

Simon, Norma, Hanukkah. New York: Crowell Co., 1966.

Shapp, Martha and Charles, Let's Find Out About Jewish Holidays.   .
    New York: Franklin Watts, Inc., 1971.

Christmas

Barth, Edna, Holly, Reindeer and Colored Lights. New York:
    The Seabury Press, 1971.

Baum, L. Frank, A Kidnapped Santa Claus. New York: The Bobbs-
    Merrill Co., 1969.

Belting, Natalia, Christmas Folk. New York: Holt, Rinehart &
    Winston, 1969.

Borland, Hal, The Youngest Shepherd. New York: J. B. Lippincott,
    1962.

Bradford, Roark, How Come Christmas. New York: Harper & Row, 1948.

Buck, Pearl, The Christmas Ghost. New York: The John Day Co., 1968.

Coopersmith, Jerome, A Chanukah Fable for Christmas. New York:
   G. P. Putnam's Sons, 1969.

Erik Blegnad, The Conscience Pudding. Coward-McCann, Inc., 1970.

Estes, Eleanor, The Coat Hanger Christmas Tree. New York:
   Attenum, 1973.

Johnson, Lois S., Christmas Stories Round the World. New York:
   Rand McNally and Co., 1970.

Lenski, Lois, Lois Lenski's Christmas Stories. New York: J. B.
   Lippincott, 1968.

McGinley, Phyllis, A Wreath of Christmas Legends. New York:
   MacMillan Co., 1969.

McGinley, Phyllis, How Mrs. Santa Claus Saved Christmas.
   New York: Lippincott Co., 1963.

McGinley, Phyllis, Mince Pie and Mistletoe. New York: Lippincott, 1959.

Patterson, Lillie, Christmas Feasts and Festivals. Illinois:
   Garrard Publishing Co., 1968.

Patterson, Lillie, Christmas in America. Illinois: Garrard Publishing
   Co., 1969.

Patterson, Lillie, Christmas in Britain and Scandinavia. Illinois:
   Garrard Publishing Co., 1970.

Purdy, Susan, Christmas Decorations for You to Make. New York:
   Lippincott Co., 1965.

Pauli, Hertha, America's First Christmas. New York: Ives
   Washburn, Inc., 1962.

Robbins, Ruth, Baboushka and the Three Kings. California:
   Parnassus Press, 1960.

Sechrist, Elizabeth Hough, Christmas Everywhere – A Book of
   Christmas Customs of Many Lands. (Revised Edition) Philadelphia:
   Macrae Smith Co., 1962.

Todd, Mary Fidelis, The Juggler of Notre Dame. New York: McGraw-Hill Book Co., Inc., 1954.

Tudor, Tasha, Becky's Christmas. New York: The Viking Press, 1966.

Wanning, Elizabeth, The Christmas Mouse. New York: Holt Rinehart & Winston, 1959.

Wernecke, Herbert, Celebrating Christmas Around the World. Philadelphia: The Westminister Press, 1962.

New Year's Day

Aliki, New Year's Day. New York: Crowell Co., 1967.

Groh, Lynn, A Holiday Book, New Year's Day. Illinois: Garrard, 1964.

Janice, Little Bear's New Year's Party. New York: Lothrop, Lee & Shepard Co., 1973.

Johnson, Lois, Happy New Year Round the World. New York: Rand McNally, 1966.

Liange, Yen, Happy New Year. New York: J. B. Lippincott, 1961.

Mariana, Miss Flora McFlimsey and the Baby New Year. New York: Lothrop Lee & Shepard Co., Inc., 1951.

Shapp, Martha and Charles, Let's Find Out About New Year's Day. New York: Franklin Watts, Inc., 1968.

Pun Week

Rees, Ennis, Pun Fun. New York: Schuman, 1965.

Birthdays

Brewton, Sara and John, Birthday Candles Burning Bright. New York: MacMillan, 1960.

Johnson, Lois, Happy Birthdays Round the World. New York: Rand McNally, 1963.

Patterson, Lillie, *A Holiday Book, Birthdays*. Illinois: Garrard, 1965.

Schatz, Letta, *When Will My Birthday Be?* New York: McGraw, 1962.

Groundhog Day

Weise, Kurt, *The Groundhog and His Shadow*. New York: Viking Press, 1959.

Holland, Joyce, *Gertie Groundhog*. Minnesota: T. S. Denison & Co., 1963.

Abraham Lincoln's Birthday

Bulla, Clyde Robert, *Lincoln's Birthday*. New York: Crowell Co., 1965.

Cary, Barbara, *Meet Abraham Lincoln*. New York: Random House, 1965.

Hays, Wilma Pitchford, *Abe Lincoln's Birthday*. New York: Coward-McCann, Inc., 1961.

Miers, Earl Schenck, *That Lincoln Boy*. New York: World Publishing Co., 1968.

Nathan, Adele, *Lincoln's America*. New York: Grosset & Dunlap, 1961.

Valentine's Day

Bianco, Pamela, *The Valentine Party*. New York: Lippincott Co., 1965.

Bulla, Clyde R., *Saint Valentine's Day*. New York: Crowell Co., 1965.

Bulla, Clyde R., *Valentine Cat*. New York: Crowell Co., 1959.

Guilfoils, Elizabeth, *Valentine's Day*. Illinois: Garrard Co., 1965.

Hays, Wilma P., *Story of Valentine*. New York: Coward Co., 1956.

Lovelace, Maud H., *Valentine Box*. New York: Crowell Co., 1966.

Milhous, Katherine, Appolonia's Valentine. New York: Scribner
    & Sons, 1954.

Schultz, Gwen, Blue Valentine. New York: Morrow & Co., 1965.

George Washington's Birthday

Bulla, Clyde, Washington's Birthday. New York: Crowell, 1967.

Hays, Wilma Pitchford, George Washington's Birthday. New York:
    Coward, 1963.

Heilbroner, Joan, Meet George Washington. New York: Random
    House, 1964.

Holland, Janice, Hello, George Washington. Nashville: Abingdon,
    1958.

Judson, Clara, George Washington. Chicago: Follett, 1961.

Koral, Bella, George Washington. New York: Random House, 1954.

Lowitz, Anson, General George The Great. Minneapolis: Lerner
    Publishing, 1968.

Norman, Gertrude, A Man Named Washington. New York: Putnam's,
    1960.

Dental Health Week

Buchheimer, Naomi, Let's Go to the Dentist. New York: Putnam's,
    1959.

Jubelier, Ruth, About Jack's Dental Check Up. Illinois: Melmont, 1959.

Kessler, Ethel and Leon, Our Tooth Story. New York: Dodd, Mead
    & Co., 1972.

Schloat, G. Warren, Your Wonderful Teeth. New York: Scribner's
    Sons, 1954.

Shay, Arthur, What It's Like To Be A Dentist. Chicago: Reilly & Lee,
    1972.

Black History Week

Fisher, Aileen, and Rabe, Olive, Human Rights Day. New York: Crowell Co., 1966.

Jackson, Florence, The Black Man in America. New York: Watts, Inc., 1973.

Jordan, June, Dry Victories. New York: Holt, Rinehart & Winston, 1972.

Miers, Earl S., The Story of the American Negro. New York: Grosset & Dunlap, 1965.

Young, Margaret, The First Book of American Negroes. New York: Watts, Inc., 1966.

Saint Patrick's Day

Cantwell, Mary, Saint Patrick's Day. New York: Thomas Y. Crowell Co., 1967.

Janice, Little Bear Marches in the St. Patrick's Day Parade. New York: Lothrop, Lee & Shepard Co., Inc., 1967.

First Day of Spring

Anglund, Joan Walch, Spring is a New Beginning. New York: Harcourt Brace, 1963.

Banks, Marjorie Ann, How We Celebrate Our Spring Holidays. New York: Benetic Co., 1961.

Blus, Joan, It's Spring, She Said. New York: Knopf Co., 1968.

Carrick, Carol, Swamp Spring. New York: MacMillan, 1969.

Craig, Jean, Spring is Like the Morning. New York: Putnam Co., 1965.

Epstein, Samuel, Spring Holidays. Illinois: Garrard Co., 1964.

Fox, Charles P., When Spring Comes. New York: Reilly & Lee, 1964.

Gay, Zhenya, Nicest Time of Year. Viking Press, 1960.

Jackson, Jacqueline, Spring Song: Verses and Music for Children. Ohio: Kent State Univ. Press, 1969.

Johnson, Crockett, Will Spring Be Early or Will Spring Be Late? New York: Crowell Co., 1959.

Kumin, Maxine W., Spring Things. New York: Putnam Co., 1961.

Kuskin, Karla, The Bear Who Saw Spring. New York: Harper Row Co., 1961.

Lenski, Lois, Spring Is Here. New York: Walck Co., 1945.

Lindgreen, Astrid, Springtime in Noisy Village. Viking Press, 1966.

Luckhardt, Mildred, Spring World, Awake! Nashville: Abingdon Press, 1970.

Miles, Betty, A Day of Spring. New York: Knopf Co., 1970.

North, Sterling, Hurry Spring. New York: Dutton Co., 1966.

Shapp, Charles and Martha, Let's Find Out About Spring. New York: Watts, 1963.

Sterling, Dorothy, Spring is Here. New York: Doubleday, 1964.

Weggant, Noemi, It's Spring. New York: Westminister, 1969.

Zion, Gene, Really Spring. New York: Harper Row, 1956.

National Wildlife Week

Graham, Ada and Frank, Wildlife Rescue. New York: Cowles, 1970.

Mason, George, The Wildlife of North America. New York: Hastings House, 1966.

Van Dersal, William, Wildlife for America. New York: Walck, Inc., 1949.

April Fool's Day

Tina, Dorothy, April Fool's Day. Chicago: Follett Co., 1969.

Earth Week

Chester, Michael, Stop Air Pollution. New York: Putnam's, 1968.

Elliott, Sarah, Our Dirty Air. New York: Messner, 1971.

Hungerford, Harold, Ecology. Chicago: Children's Press, 1971.

Leaf, Munro, Who Cares? I Do. New York: Lippincott Co., 1971.

Milgrom, Harry, ABC of Ecology. New York: MacMillan, 1972.

Podendorf, Illa, Every Day is Earth Day. Chicago: Children's Press, 1971.

Pringle, Laurence, The Only Earth We Have. London: Collier-MacMillan, 1969.

Shuttlesworth, Dorothy, Clean Air - Sparkling Water. New York: Doubleday, 1968.

Tannenbaum, Beulah, and Stillman, Myra, Clean Air. New York: MacMillan, 1973.

Easter

Armour, Richard, The Adventures of Egbert the Easter Egg. New York: McGraw-Hill Book Co., 1965.

Barth, Edna, Lilies, Rabbits, Painted Eggs: The Story of Easter Symbols. New York: Seabury, 1970.

Bianco, Pamela, The Look-Inside Easter Egg. New York: Henry Z. Walck, Inc., 1952.

Budd, Lillian, Tekla's Easter. New York: Rand McNally & Co., 1962.

Coskey, Evelyn, Easter Eggs for Everyone. Nashville: Abingdon, 1973.

DeJong, Meindert, The Easter Cat. New York: MacMillan, 1971.

Duvoisin, Roger, Easter Treat. New York: Alfred A. Knopf,
1954.

Fisher, Aileen, Easter. New York: Crowell, 1968.

Friedrich, Priscilla, and Otto, The Easter Bunny That Overslept.
New York: Lothrop, 1957.

Kraus, Robert, Daddy Long Ears. New York: Simon & Schuster,
1970.

Milhous, Katherine, The Egg Tree. New York: Charles Scribner's
Sons, 1950.

Prido, Pauline, Piccolina and the Easter Bells. New York:
Little, 1962.

Roser, Wilfred, Everything About Easter Bunnies. New York:
Crowell, 1973.

Thayer, Jane, The Horse With the Easter Bonnet. New York:
William Morrow & Co., 1953.

Tresselt, Alvin R., The World in the Candy Egg. Lothrop, 1967.

Watts, Franklin, Let's Find Out About Easter. Watts, 1969.

Young, Mariam, Miss Suzy's Easter Surprise. Parents Magazine Co.,
1972.

Zolotow, Charlotte, The Bunny Who Found Easter. Berkley, Calif.:
Parnassus Press, 1959.

Arbor Day

Darby, Gene, What Is A Tree, Chicago: Benefic Press, 1957.

Fisher, Aileen, Arbor Day. New York: Crowell Co., 1965.

Lauber, Patricia, Our Friend the Forest. New York: Doubleday, 1959.

Lemmon, Robert S., Junior Science Book of Trees. Illinois:
Garrard Press, 1960.

Podendorf, Illa, The True Book of Trees. Chicago: Children's Press, 1954.

Shapp, Martha and Charles, Let's Find Out About Trees. New York: Franklin Watts, 1970.

Winter, Ginny, What's In My Tree? New York: Astor Honor, Inc., 1962.

May Day

Calhoun, Mary, The Flower Mother. New York: William Morrow Co., 1972.

Hays, Wilma Pitchford, May Day for Samoset. New York: Coward McCann, Inc., 1968.

Mariana, Miss Flora McFlimsey's May Day. New York: Lothrop, Lee & Shepard Co., 1969.

Tina, Dorothy, May Day. New York: Crowell Co., 1967.

Mother's Day

Phelan, Mary Kay, Mother's Day. New York: Crowell Co., 1965.

Flag Day

Crouthers, David, Flags of American History. New Jersey: Hammond, 1962.

Freeman, Mae Blacker, Stars and Stripes. New York: Random House, 1964.

Georgiady, Nicholas and Romano, Louis, Our Country's Flag. New York: Follett, 1963.

Glick, Carl, and Ollie Rogers, The Story of Our Flag. New York: Putnam's, 1964.

Parrish, Thomas, The American Flag. New York: Simon & Schuster, 1973.

Rees, Elinor, About Our Flag. Chicago: Melmont, 1960.

Tina, Dorothy, Flag Day. New York: Crowell Co., 1965.

Waller, Leslie, Our Flag. New York: Holt, Rinehart & Winston, 1960.

Father's Day

Puner, Helen, Daddys – What They Do All Day. New York: Lothrop, 1946.

Schauffler, Robert Haven, The Days We Celebrate, Vol. 4. New York: Dodd Mead Co., 1954.

Stewart, Robert, The Daddy Book. New York: American Heritage Press, 1972.

First Day of Summer

Burningham, John, Seasons. New York: Bobbs Merrill Co., 1970.

Burton, Leslie, Parade of Seasons. New York: Platt, 1971.

Cole, William, Poems for Seasons and Celebrations. New York: World, 1961.

Darby, Gene, What Is A Season. New York: Benefic, 1960.

Dow, Katherine, My Time of Year. New York: Walck, 1961.

Farjean, Eleanor, Around the Seasons. New York: Walck, 1969.

Goudey, Alice E., The Day We Saw The Sun Come Up. New York: Charles Scribner's and Sons, 1961.

Low, Alice, Summer. New York: Random House, 1963.

Kane, Henry B., Four Seasons in the Woods. New York: Knopf, 1968.

Podendorf, Illa, True Book of Seasons, New York: Children's Press, 1972.

Radlaver, Ruth S., *About Four Seasons and Five Senses*.
   New York: Melmont, 1960.

Schick, Eleanor, *City In The Summer*. New York: MacMillan, 1969.

Shannon, Terry, *Come Summer, Come Winter*. New York:
   Whitman, 1956.

Zolotow, Charlotte, *Summer Is*. New York: Abelard, 1967.

Fourth of July

Graves, Charles, *Fourth of July*. Illinois: Garrard Publishing Co.,
   1963.

Phelan, Mary Kay, *The Fourth of July*. New York: Crowell Co.,
   1966.

SELECTED TEACHER REFERENCES

Fiarotta, Phyllis, Sticks and Stones and Ice Cream Cones.
  New York: Workman Publishing Co., 1973.

Gilbreath, Alice, Making Costumes for Parties, Plays and Holidays.
  New York: William Morrow & Co., 1974.

Hark, Mildred, and Noel McQueen, Special Plays for Special Days.
  Boston: Plays, Inc., 1947.

Krythe, Maymie R., All About American Holidays. New York:
  Harper and Brothers, 1962.

Larrick, Nancy, More Poetry for Holidays. Illinois: Garrard
  Publishing Co., 1973.

Larrick, Nancy, Poetry for Holidays. Illinois: Garrard Publishing
  Co., 1966.

McGovern, Ann, Why It's A Holiday. New York: Random House, 1960.

McSpadden, J. Walker, The Book of Holidays. New York:
  Crowell Co., 1958.

Newman, Dana, The Teacher's Almanack. New York: The
  Center for Applied Research in Education, Inc., 1973.